PRAISE FOR

THE CORPORATE SOCIAL MIND

"More and more companies are debating what constitutes a good purpose in a complex world. This book provides practical help in anchoring these debates in a systemic view of corporate responsibility towards society. Studying the cases in the book and following the authors' framework of traits of companies with a corporate social mind will add depth to these debates and will help avoid the trap of corporate social responsibility activities that are unconnected to the core of the business."

—PROFESSOR JOHANNES MEIER, PhD, board member, NEW WORK SE, Mercator Foundation, and UNICEF Germany

"An important subject, the right authors, a great book."

—DR. KNUT BERGMANN, Head of Communications and Head of Berlin Office, German Economic Institute

"*The Corporate Social Mind* is a perfect primer for companies looking to reimagine their social purpose and engage meaning-fully with movement organisations. I highly recommend this book for any leader seeking to better understand how to survive and thrive in a world where new economic systems are emerging."

—CHARMIAN LOVE, Cofounder and Chair, B Lab UK

"*The Corporate Social Mind* is timely, refreshing, and actionable. Derrick Feldmann and Michael Alberg-Seberich ask the relevant questions and give voice to those who start to act. A must-read for everyone who decides to *do* and not just talk about social impact."

—JOHANNA MAIR, PhD, Professor of Organization, Strategy, and Leadership, Hertie School; Hewlett Foundation Visiting Scholar, Stanford Center on Philanthropy and Civil Society; Academic Editor, Stanford Social Innovation Review

"Given today's challenges, we all need to take a hard look at what it's going to take to scale impact and drive true change. Derrick's and Michael's book inspires today's leaders to take a fresh and holistic look at current approaches to social impact. At the Ad Council, we see firsthand how this formula—integrating corporate philanthropy, innovation and marketing, and communications—can create powerful ways to engage the public but also drive employee engagement and business results. This book will inspire and motivate all of us to do more."

—LISA SHERMAN, President and CEO, Ad Council

"*The Corporate Social Mind* is a timely contribution to an important debate about the responsibility of business. Its examples are engaging, the management practices it presents are inspiring, and the questions it raises are important for the future role of business in society."

—JOHANNES HUTH, Partner and Head of KKR Europe, Middle East, and Africa

"For 20 years, Chief Executives for Corporate Purpose (CECP) has been empowering leading companies to build a better world through business. With *The Corporate Social Mind*, Derrick Feldmann and Michael Alberg-Seberich have crafted a must-read guidebook, enhanced by powerful case studies, for anyone interested in clarifying the often murky space between social challenges and corporate strategy."

—**DARYL BREWSTER**, CEO, Chief Executives for Corporate Purpose

"An increasing number of people expect private businesses to not only maximize shareholder value but also to take over a broader, quasi-governmental responsibility. Some companies are already adopting this new role by leading social change and thereby shaping the future of our human civilization. This book is a brilliant collection of best practices and an excellent summary of the state of the art of the field. At the same time, the book opens up a space for a critical discussion about these recent developments and stresses the importance of collective reflection. A must-read for every conscious individual in our economies, regardless of management level."

—**LAURA MARIE EDINGER-SCHONS**, PhD, Professor of Corporate Social Responsibility, University of Mannheim Business School; Cofounder, Digital Social Innovation Lab

"An invaluable tool for companies awakening to a higher purpose. *The Corporate Social Mind* offers a unique, multidisciplinary perspective on delivering social impact authentic to your brand and values."

—**KATIE HUNT-MORR**, Director, Virgin Unite

"For many years we suffered from the social effects of the American shareholder value doctrine. Now, we have Greta. For all these reasons, this book comes as an important handbook with recipes and illustrations of responsible behavior in small and large enterprises at a time of massive challenges for society and companies that should be significant contributors to our sustainability at large."

—DR. STEPHAN GOETZ, Managing Partner,
goetzpartners Corporate Finance

"My philosophy has always been to link sustainability to business issues in order to create value (social, environmental, economic) for everyone. This can only succeed with perfect alignment between who you are, what you say, and what you effectively do. This book is an incredible demonstration of this. An inspiring reading to take action!"

—FANNY FREMONT, Executive Director,
Responsible Mica Initiative

"Derrick and Michael have presented a thoughtful, easy-to-consume guide for how business leaders can approach not just incorporating social impact into their companies, but how they can make it central to their strategies. *The Corporate Social Mind* broadens the focus on how business delivers societal impact beyond the critical CSR function and makes it an imperative for all leaders."

—RACHEL HUTCHISSON, Vice President of Corporate
Citizenship & Philanthropy, Blackbaud, Inc.

"In family enterprises, nurturing social minds is part of our DNA across generational boundaries. As the world accelerates and inequality rises, we need to integrate new KPIs to provide society with a more virtuous and better-balanced economic model. Derrick and Michael are providing us with an invaluable toolset of lived experiences and best practices to stretch our minds and provoke 'social change from the inside out.' Their book is a must-read for every learning family."

—OLIVIER DE RICHOUFFTZ, President, Business Families Foundation

"The Corporate Social Mind is clear, in language and content, filled with sound advice and practical guidance. The call to action is also very timely and urgent: corporate social values should require companies to be present, be practiced, be supportive of society, and be authentic. It provides good guidance for companies to identify the right assets to contribute to addressing societal issues. It offers a mindset shift for effective leaders."

—MARIA SERENA PORCARI, Managing Director, Dynamo Academy Social Enterprise

"The management of a company's purpose and social engagement is a crucial leadership task these days. Derrick's and Michael's book is a good repository for concrete examples of this kind of leadership on various levels of management. Their nine traits should be part of the toolbox of modern-day businesses."

—BRIGITTE LAMMERS, Partner, Egon Zehnder

THE
CORPORATE
SOCIAL
MIND

THE
CORPORATE
SOCIAL
MIND

HOW
COMPANIES
LEAD
SOCIAL CHANGE
FROM THE
INSIDE OUT

DERRICK FELDMANN
MICHAEL ALBERG-SEBERICH

**FAST
COMPANY**
Press

Fast Company Press
New York, New York
www.fastcompanypress.com

This work is being published under the Fast Company Press imprint by an exclusive arrangement with *Fast Company*. *Fast Company* and the *Fast Company* logo are registered trademarks of Mansueto Ventures, LLC. The Fast Company Press logo is a wholly owned trademark of Mansueto Ventures, LLC.

Distributed by Greenleaf Book Group

For ordering information or special discounts for bulk purchases, please contact Greenleaf Book Group at PO Box 91869, Austin, TX 78709, 512.891.6100.

Design and composition by Greenleaf Book Group
Cover design by Greenleaf Book Group

Publisher's Cataloging-in-Publication data is available.

Print ISBN: 978-1-7343248-0-8

eBook ISBN: 978-1-7343248-1-5

Part of the Tree Neutral® program, which offsets the number of trees consumed in the production and printing of this book by taking proactive steps, such as planting trees in direct proportion to the number of trees used: www.treeneutral.com

TreeNeutral

Printed in the United States of America on acid-free paper

20 21 22 23 24 25   10 9 8 7 6 5 4 3 2 1

First Edition

To Bis, Paige, and Blair. Thank you for allowing me to do this work every single day. Your love, patience, and support are both overwhelming and heartwarming. I couldn't ask for anything more.

—DF

To my son Johann, who reminded me the whole time how important it is to finish this book. To my family, without whom this book never would have been possible. Thank you!

—MAS

CONTENTS

PREFACE

....

We are from two different worlds—literally and figuratively. Derrick Feldmann is a researcher and advisor based in the United States who has been in the social issue and movement space with companies and causes for 20 years, specifically focused on understanding, engaging, and communicating with the public to help them get involved in social issues.

Michael Alberg-Seberich is a researcher and advisor based in Europe who has been in the social issue and impact space with companies and foundations for more than 25 years, specifically focused on designing social impact approaches and strategies with multinational companies, family businesses, foundations, and corporate philanthropy and corporate social responsibility teams.

But what we share is very important. We both work on social issues and helping companies leverage their assets for change.

Ever since we met more than 15 years ago, we've been in heated debates about the importance of social issues and their impact—Michael from the social responsibility side and Derrick from the marketing and communications side. Any time we are in each other's country, it's common for us to meet over dinner (and many coffees) and to end our long discussions with valid points on the importance of both sides. We agree that to make real progress, a company has to move beyond whether one way is right or wrong and simply work together closely with civil society, government, and other companies, even though it's sometimes hard.

In our work together, we've realized something else, too. Both functions—the corporate social responsibility, social innovation, and impact team, and the marketing and communications team—lack an understanding of each other's work and some of the fundamental approaches to how each should engage in campaigns, moments, and movements.

In addition, new trends in corporate social issue engagement have been combining efforts of both functions, so that corporate social impact work and marketing/communications are both asking one another for data, insights, and strategies in order to be able to address social issues. This type of social issue involvement can be a key area for internal collaboration and innovation.

Therefore, we set out to create a book that would allow people from both sides to move beyond their own ways of thinking and operating and come together to address social issues through a mindset that embeds certain traits into the daily work of companies beyond just role and function. While this enhanced mindset redefines the company's approach to social issue engagement, it also removes internal barriers to addressing social issues with consumers, communities, stakeholders, and the public. It creates a collaborative space for something new with business and social impact.

The Corporate Social Mind is intentionally set up to be referenced during internal conversations about values and purpose, public social issue engagement, consumer-based marketing campaigns with causes and social issues, and leadership development programs for corporate employees that involve or incorporate community engagement methods.

The book provides a snapshot of many actual global examples and stories from companies working with this different mindset. Some of these companies you know, and some will be new to you. We focused on companies and initiatives—regardless of their size, location, and reach—that are making an impact on the issues they address. This is for all our benefit, because working on social issues requires insights from all types of companies and from all parts of the world.

We also recognize the bias we bring to this book due to our focus on global companies that are primarily European and United States businesses. We know more cases around the world can be shared among leaders striving for deeper social issue impact, and we hope this book will help bring those examples forward for us to promote, highlight, and use to ignite new conversations and even potentially create new traits for the corporate social mind.

In trying to help both sides understand a new mindset for addressing social issues, we realize that our social issue expert/research colleagues will unlikely be satisfied by our coverage of certain elements in the book that we could not go into deeply enough. Our intent was to introduce a new cultural and strategic approach to social issue engagement by companies. As companies get better at incorporating this new mindset, we will have other opportunities outside of *The Corporate Social Mind* for exploration. Finally, we intend to develop new resources and case studies that allow for deeper dialogue in the future at thecorporatesocialmind.com.

This is a great time for you as a leader to address social issues with a new mindset—a Corporate Social Mind. So, welcome, and thank you for reading. Don't forget to join the conversation using **#corpsocialmind** and visit **thecorporatesocialmind.com** for new/updated resources.

NOTE FROM
DERRICK FELDMANN

....

I can remember stories from when I was growing up of what it would mean to own a business and make money. From parents to early mentors, people would talk about the fulfillment you get for yourself and your family when you can buy that house, get that new car, or start checking things off your bucket list. This, as so many people would say, is when you know you have, in their words, "made it."

I bought into that notion.

In college, I would constantly think about living out this dream that others defined as success. I would present ideas to anyone who would listen. As does any aspiring entrepreneur, I thought I could create a viable business and then, somehow, it would take off and make everything possible.

However, as I became more educated about the world's problems and began to have more experiences outside the comfortable bubble I was used to, I realized that there was more to business than what others were telling me. Although I understood the need to make money, I decided not to let money define the role I saw business taking in society. I slowly began to see that when I bought something, experienced a service, or, quite frankly, even watched a movie or advertisement, companies behind those things can and do have a powerful position in our society and culture.

When I buy a burrito and understand a complex food system or when I eat a piece of chocolate and, as a consumer, am informed about the life of a cocoa farmer and the impact of the product on so many others besides just myself, I am the beneficiary of knowledge that I never would have had without the willingness of a company to infuse a social mindset into their decisions to educate the consumer.

This is an example of the convergence of business and society.

NOTE FROM
MICHAEL ALBERG-SEBERICH

I never thought I would be co-authoring a book with Derrick, especially a book that incorporates corporate marketing and communications about social impact. But it is clear from my own experiences in my work with so many companies that corporate marketing and communications is clearly intertwined with social impact: In order to be effective today, we cannot avoid working together within the company while also expecting bigger outcomes externally.

My father, a trained industrial engineer and first-generation IT consultant in the 1960s and 1970s in Germany, has been the formative person in my life when it comes to business. He was the person who encouraged me to study what interested me. He was always confident that curiosity and an entrepreneurial attitude would drive a career.

My career started out in the nonprofit and philanthropy sector. From the beginning, my path was about creating positive impact for society. I took this interest into my work with foundations, companies, and investment vehicles at Wider Sense, the consultancy and think tank I cofounded and currently work for. In this work it became obvious that just a *good* corporate social responsibility, corporate citizenship, or corporate philanthropy strategy, or a *good* way to measure your impact is by far not enough for a company to support social change. I always dreamt of moving these business disciplines out of their silos. In the conversations with Derrick it became clear that brands, communication, and marketing can play a crucial role in enhancing social change driven by business. It also became clear that we should consider this approach as a mindset within a company. This book talks about how some companies have done this and how every manager can do this. It is based on a mindset that my father shared with me—that a business as a whole, from innovation to marketing, can drive positive social change in our societies when it is integrated into the way we do the actual work.

Combining Our Voices to
Move Society toward Change

C ompanies can move our minds and hearts when they help us understand complex issues, or teach us what happens when we take ownership of a failure and build on it for success in the future, or when they push us beyond our own biases to consider something new and unique that is a result of something more than just consuming a good or product.

To help businesses develop this power, *The Corporate Social Mind* will define the traits, values, and industry standards companies must reflect and operate with to be authentic and successful for the people they affect (internally and externally) and the societies they seek to change.

Companies can be the beating heart behind so many of our issues today—if they choose to be. And we, as consumers and professionals, have an opportunity to engage alongside these companies. Our combined voices can truly move society toward change.

Social change comes in many forms, but it is generally agreed that in today's complex world, all sectors contributing together yield greater probability of sustained societal impact than when a brand, government agency, or even a nonprofit goes it alone. The old sayings are true: It is better together, and no one is an island unto themselves.

TODAY'S SOCIAL BUSINESS

More and more businesses today are taking action and being socially conscious. Research continues to reinforce the position that business is vital to solving society's problems. However, though research supports the need for and efficacy of companies to be socially minded, even more (and less acknowledged) reasons exist for companies to engage in society's challenges—reasons that go far beyond the bottom line. They include some internally focused reasons, such as:

- Conducting ethical business practices so as not to harm societies and our world.

- Responding to pressure by shareholders, consumers, and governments to meet certain standards or contribute to the greater good of an industry or citizenry.

- Building a reputation that garners higher brand affinity and loyalty to companies with the needs of society embedded into their internal and external practices.

- Living up to the company's values that contribute to a workplace culture based on purpose rather than only profit.

- Infusing executive leadership interests, experience, and (positive) biases toward certain populations, social issues, relationships, and communities. At certain times in some family businesses, this means fulfilling personal values in the process of directing company resources.

Beyond the interests of the company or internally focused reasons, communities, consumers, societies, and governments push companies to engage in social issues for additional, externally focused reasons, such as:

- Society now expects business to account for the environmental, social, and economic impact one's business has on the planet, the locale in which the company operates, or the people that live, work, and play within the company's presence. Essentially, we must consider the ripple effects that developing, producing, and selling goods and services have on others.

- Employees seek companies that advance societies rather than deter, ignore, or aggravate them. At the same time, these employees seek employers that do the right thing by their own people and communities via respectable wages and earnings, supporting safe and healthy workplaces, and reinforcing proper behavior for all.

- Consumer consumption practices have changed to be more consciously driven, resulting in companies meeting new consumer interests, societal expectations, and safety issues with their products and services. Balancing consumer demands and convenience with societal issues and expectations—along with corporate product and service methods—is a thoughtful practice that needs consistent iteration.

- Investment opportunities have increased for businesses that focus on social issues along with products and services that fulfill a consumer/business demand. Private investors with a goal of meeting society's challenges are growing in number, and such opportunities for companies of all sizes are continuing to demand new approaches in dealing with social issues and the environment.

- Businesses of all sizes are looking to connect more of their corporate values with the communities they impact. In addition, as business becomes an even more active player in social good, future generations of owners will be dealing with even greater pressures to engage in societal impact projects and initiatives.

All of these reasons contribute to a company's decision to engage, but each alone isn't a reason to make society's challenges a priority for any business. Rather, companies that make a conscious decision to infuse the good of society into their business do so in an effort to make business and society work together in a symbiotic relationship to fulfill the needs of individuals, families, and the places we call home.

EVOLUTION: FROM CORPORATE PHILANTHROPY TO SOCIETAL IMPACT

The phenomenon of business working on social issues has evolved through history as changes in culture, society, and generational perspectives have led to a more deliberate and holistic approach to societal change. These shifts have been triggered by many levers: conflict, natural disasters, new technology development, and global financial market changes, among others.

This has meant moving beyond just the "people, planet, and profit" approach that is often talked about in the field.

Each evolutionary moment of corporate citizenship has demanded greater focus and outcomes, bringing more and more stakeholders together to combat society's challenges through the use of company assets. We view this progression as four distinct moments, each characterized by a certain focus:

MOMENT 1: CORPORATE PHILANTHROPY

Giving financial resources or human capital in the form of volunteers and in-kind programs through a coordinated company plan. This encompasses other efforts to bring together doers and dollars.

MOMENT 2: CORPORATE SOCIAL RESPONSIBILITY

Creating programs and initiatives that support the development of proper environmental and supply chain efforts to address the impact products, practices, goods, and services have on society at large.

MOMENT 3: SOCIAL GOOD

Blurring the boundaries between sectors to address society's issues via innovative approaches, incorporating customized business and financial practices that leverage a social outcome. From B Corps to impact investing, these approaches break down the historical silos of business and nonprofit.

MOMENT 4: SOCIETAL IMPACT

Taking a holistic approach to assets and applying methods of marketing, communication, investment, partnership, collaboratives, and social leadership to issues. This infuses societal impact approaches into all levels of business that are measured, analyzed, and coordinated to advance society.

A COMPANY'S ROLE

We often see companies assume particular roles when dealing with social issues. The roles often change over time and can alter based on the approach to assess engagement the company takes relative to a particular issue. We can define these roles succinctly, as follows:

- **The Spontaneous** provide opportunistic financial donations that do not have a specific strategic focus.

- **The Donors** show a somewhat diluted focus and short-term resource planning with donations directed toward nongovernmental organizations (NGOs).

- **The Committed** address some long-term challenges and have allocated appropriate resources for this purpose, yet are not explicitly oriented toward results and impact.

- **The Strategists** display a focused strategy and purpose and have a clear orientation toward results and impact.

- **The Integrated** fully assimilate corporate citizenship into the company's daily business and social value chain.[1]

WHAT IS A CORPORATE SOCIAL MIND?

A corporate social mind is an approach to doing business. A business with a corporate social mind embodies traits that incorporate social impact into every aspect of the company's existence. By definition, a company with a corporate social mind infuses social outcomes into everything from supply chain to product/service intelligence to delivery, marketing, communications, and beyond.

A business with a corporate social mind reflects the following traits:

TRAIT 1: A BUSINESS WITH A CORPORATE SOCIAL MIND DECIDES WITH SOCIETY IN MIND

Leadership has the issue of societal benefit on the table in all its decisions, all the time. Decisions are never made without asking the question: In what ways does this decision affect the company, people, society, and the environment?

TRAIT 2: A BUSINESS WITH A CORPORATE SOCIAL MIND LIVES ITS VALUES

A company's values express every employee's commitment to caring for the community and working toward an improved world. Employees at all levels consider social good as a vital part of their company's existence and practice these values in their daily work.

TRAIT 3: A BUSINESS WITH A CORPORATE SOCIAL MIND USES RESOURCES FOR SOCIETY'S BENEFIT

Companies use their intellectual, social, financial, and emotional capital to drive ideas that advance societal progress.

TRAIT 4: A BUSINESS WITH A CORPORATE SOCIAL MIND LISTENS BEFORE ACTING

Companies listen to society before driving innovation and implementation. Societal benefit, impact, and desires are heard and understood before actions are taken and prior to designing and executing new products, services, and solutions.

TRAIT 5: A BUSINESS WITH A CORPORATE SOCIAL MIND HAS A SOCIAL VOICE

Along with transparency, having an authentic voice on societal issues is vital to ensuring consumers, the public, and stakeholders understand a company's views. Having a voice on an issue doesn't mean the issue must be relatable to the company's product; the issue may simply affect people within the company's community.

TRAIT 6: A BUSINESS WITH A CORPORATE SOCIAL MIND LEADS SOCIAL COLLECTIVES

Social collectives are cohorts or a network or group of companies that share common purpose and/or outcomes for a social issue. Companies lead and engage by driving the agenda of social-issue collectives. These collectives include representation from all the sectors (private, public, and nonprofit) that could make issue-related change happen.

TRAIT 7: A BUSINESS WITH A CORPORATE SOCIAL MIND MEASURES SOCIAL IMPACT

Companies measure the impact of their decisions on all aspects of society, as well as on their business. Moreover, a culture of transparency in reporting finances, societal impact, product development, and impact on people and the planet is intentional and pervasive.

TRAIT 8: A BUSINESS WITH A CORPORATE SOCIAL MIND INNOVATES FOR SOCIAL GOOD

All innovations address both a consumer/business and a social need. The company always applies its services, knowledge, and consumer insights to create or enhance something that benefits both itself and society.

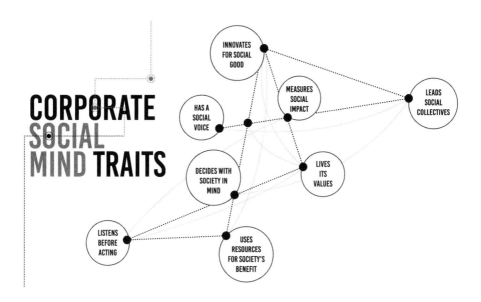

We know that companies that infuse societal impact into their business models perform better and are more profitable. The key is to focus on making sure all these traits work together simultaneously as they are embedded into the company's operations and decision-making structures. Management cannot assume these traits will function concurrently or find their own paths of connection.

All this is a dialogue between different values and different stakeholders. An ever-growing portion of today's consumers shop with their conscience, becoming intensely loyal to (and advocates for) a company whose values align with their own. Many workers now consider a potential employer's social-good efforts when seeking and/or remaining in a job. Most significantly, the public generally understands that we cannot achieve sustainable social change unless companies get involved—and they need our support to do so.

Let's get started by using a different mindset for your work in society.

CHAPTER 1

Trait 1: A Corporate Social Mind
Decides with Society in Mind

In a business with a corporate social mind, leadership ensures that societal benefit is on the table for all decisions, all the time. Decisions are never made without asking one vital question: How does this decision affect company, people, society, and the environment?

Adam Smith, credited as the father of capitalism, recognized that moral actions are part of human nature. "How selfish soever man may be supposed," he said, "there are evidently some principles in his nature, which interest him in the fortune of others, and render their happiness necessary to him . . ."[1] While Smith would be pleased with the overwhelming number of company executives who agree with him today, how many are truly putting their social principles into practice?

An examination of your own decision-making processes is imperative to embedding a true social ethos throughout your company.

FOCUS

Leaders who are responsible for decision-making processes can use this chapter to incorporate society into their management practices. Specifically, we will discuss the answers to these questions:

- When the team makes a decision, how can we incorporate and support society in that decision?
- When deciding on the best strategy to meet company goals, how will we help others understand how the approach kept society in mind?
- What is an effective decision-making process for a company with a corporate social mind?

TRAIT 1 IN ACTION

Every entrepreneur and business leader has to make hard choices regarding their company's operations, people, and approaches to reaching key performance indicators (KPIs). Facing and responding to these challenges is what gives them the experience to lead and garner support from their employees, partners, and the consumers who buy their products and services.

Their decisions can also support what society and people within their communities desire and need to advance. Any decision operating in a silo without society in mind is one that runs counter to the symbiotic relationship companies have with the people in their communities. After all, companies depend on consumers' livelihoods to reach most of their own KPIs.

Keeping society in mind requires empathy, argue the authors of "The Role of Social Cognition and Decision Making" in *The Royal Society:*

> Successful decision making in a social setting depends on our ability to understand the intentions, emotions and beliefs of others. The mirror system allows us to understand other people's motor actions and action intentions. "Empathy" allows us to understand and share emotions and sensations with others. "Theory of mind" allows us to understand more abstract concepts such as beliefs or wishes in others . . . An important feature of decision making in a social setting concerns the interaction of reason and emotion.[2]

I can remember a situation quite clearly that illustrates the importance of this kind of deep understanding. My assistant texted me, saying that one of the leading brands in the country wanted me to fly to the West Coast for a private meeting—and soon.

It just so happened that I needed to be in the area anyway, so I said yes. But based on my history of advising companies on engaging the public (primarily millennials), I knew that one of two things had likely happened: the company had made a misstep or the public was denouncing a corporate policy or challenging the company's approach to sourcing, manufacturing, or marketing a product—and either way, the brand wasn't sure how to respond.

In this case, it was the latter.

This particular company underestimated the public's negative response to a public issue campaign around a new product. Here's the story:

The company was selling a product it claimed benefitted mental health. In what appeared to be a veiled attempt to boost sales, the company pledged to make a donation to a mental health non-profit organization for every product sold. But millennials were skeptical—and for good reason. The gift and public issue were misaligned—to get the gift, someone had to buy the product—and consumers saw the company as trying to take advantage of an issue for its own gain.

As I advised the company on where the missteps occurred and the ramifications of making decisions without consulting the beneficiary—in this case, the mental health community—it realized two important lessons: First, it's easy to make incorrect decisions when they are based on creative input without socialization. Second and more importantly, deciding without both public and private interests in mind (and putting society first) can have a powerfully negative effect on good intentions.

A Critical Question for Every Team

Being cognizant of the impact of our decisions on society puts people (employees and consumers) and communities at the table. In the process of making decisions, executives should consider society and societal benefit and, as we mentioned earlier, introduce a question during the process:

> How does this decision affect company, people, society, and
> the environment?

Decisions have ripple effects beyond the company's predetermined outcomes, and this question will help center leadership around the consequences of actions taken in the spirit of solely doing business.

Within the decision-making process, this question must be answered with insights and data before it is dismissed. This means companies must fully understand the impact of its decisions by assessing projected outcomes. This is key if the company is to exercise a true corporate social mind. Understanding a company's overall impact and complete reach is imperative to ensuring decisions do not detract from the advances of society on issues of importance. This, therefore, presents a real opportunity for companies internally focused on social responsibility and community engagement to strengthen their analysis and research teams to address their impacts on society.

In traditional corporate social responsibility and philanthropy units within companies, the focus tends to be on new initiatives or assessing the impact of the company's work against globally accepted practices and indicators. This is a starting point, however a reactive approach to assessment and not one that truly integrates forward thinking and moving the impact-on-society question into real-time decision making. It is good business planning to understand the effects of one's decisions on society *in the moment* and not in the past, after decisions have already realized outcomes and are too late to amend. Changing historical corporate behaviors and operations that have become precedent is often a challenging and onerous task—the path of most resistance.

To mitigate risks to employees, community, and society, business leaders must create a new cadence of decision making within innovative practices that caters to prompt, responsive, and iterative methods of learning, design, measurement, refinement, and scale. Sometimes these practices can be in the form of risk assessments for products, services, or goods, as in the EU REACH regulation for chemicals from 2006. However, this goes beyond typical assessments at the completion of product design into formative development and decision making at the onset of product innovation.

An example of this approach is seen in Siemens' Business to Society report, where the company effectively discusses how its new technologies and innovations impact the lives of people in the United States.[3]

An effective corporate leader with a social mindset will use a new cadence of decision making, as illustrated below.

Decision-making Process for Innovation

1. CREATE INNOVATION CONCEPT

Out of a desire to make/refine a product or service that impacts the consumption behaviors of the public, corporate leaders create a new concept for discovery, testing, and market introduction.

2. DEFINE SOCIETAL IMPACT

Once the concept is designed, the approach of the new/refined product/service is assessed for projected impact on people, society, and environment. The concept is refined to improve societal impact performance indicators.

3. DESIGN INNOVATION PROTOTYPE

Once the concept has been improved to enhance societal impact, the product/service is developed into a prototype for a market test or limited introduction into the field.

4. ASSESS SOCIETAL IMPACT

While the product/service is introduced into the market or within a targeted public distinct marketing area (DMA), the product is assessed for use and risk to society, people, and the environment concurrently with viability assessments.

5. REFINE INNOVATION PROTOTYPE

Once the field test is complete, the product is then refined to enhance its impact on the individual consumer or business. Leadership talks openly about the impact of the product on the desired market and society to determine additional refinements that improve impact on people, society, and the community holistically.

6. ASSESS SOCIETAL IMPACT

A new prototype is designed and reassessed for societal impact, and a final analysis should determine whether it will have the desired impact at scale. This deep analysis will include various methods of listening, interviewing, real-time data capturing, and predictive models. The assessment team will engage stakeholders (various audiences within society that have minimal to maximum exposure to the product/service) to understand societal benefit from the company's actions.

7. SCALE INNOVATION

Once the innovation is introduced more broadly into the consumer marketplace or general public, understanding how each community and sub-audience within new markets (DMAs) react will be imperative, given the localized differences among culture, beliefs, and consumption behaviors.

8. MONITOR SOCIETAL IMPACT

Just as a product is consistently assessed for performance-related metrics, it should also be assessed for societal impact. Societal KPIs must be designed and consistently measured to determine the long-term societal impact of decisions. Ongoing iterations may be necessary to improve impact as performance innovations are implemented.

As you can see, a corporate social mindset and culture incorporates decision making with society in mind throughout the product-development process. Assessments at any point without ongoing refinements based on feedback put the company's mission and values at risk. If the company values mutual respect and support and purports to care whether society is advanced because of its work, then this process is not just ideal—it's necessary.

How Microsoft Decides with Society in Mind

Microsoft uses a corporate social mindset when developing and designing Microsoft devices, innovating through approaches designed to measure and assess societal impact throughout the process.

Active in more than 100 countries, Microsoft's Devices Division is responsible for the ideation, design, development, manufacture, sourcing, compliance, packaging, and distribution of the company's devices and related software products. Across this process, sustainability programs are overseen by experts from many industries that bring unique vantage points into product development and societal impact. They, in turn, are supported by an internal safety, compliance, and sustainability team whose mission is to ensure flawless product compliance while promoting company values.

The internal team creates a program to understand compliance measurements and sustainability effects on society throughout the innovation cycle. While an audit management system is clearly designed to embed compliance and sustainability into the business, this additional program allows the team to make continuous supply chain improvements to alter the impacts on society.

This approach to a corporate social mindset is explained by the company itself in its sustainability and devices annual report in 2018:

> We set objectives and targets to ensure continuous improvement in our environmental performance and management systems. We value employee contributions to our initiatives. We regularly review aspects of our business activities and assess our programs, practices and goals to evaluate our progress. We proactively manage environmental risks and opportunities to identify areas where further improvements can be made. We collaborate with our suppliers to ensure that they share the same level of commitment to the continuous improvement of their environmental performance.[4]

Microsoft is also mindful of the societal implications of future innovations. Through investments, consistent monitoring, and engagement with stakeholders, it assesses emerging global trends, proposed regulations and policies, and stakeholder expectations in energy, labor rights, environmental compliance, health, product safety, and other areas. By developing its own system of measurement, the company can use a variety of data sets and relationships that will yield new insights to improve both product development and its societal impacts. Already, these data sources include the following:

- Subscriptions to regulatory tracking services
- Trainings and conferences
- Technical laboratories
- Trade and technical journals and newsletters
- Stakeholder consultations
- Meetings with peer professionals within government and industry
- Expert consultants
- Agency resources

TRAIT 1:
Design and Innovation Questions

Consider the following questions as you examine how your company addresses its social-good issue:

- How will we involve society in our design and development phases for products, goods, and services?
- How will we integrate approaches to decision making that allow us to involve key stakeholders when we spark new innovations to test and iterate?
- How can we affect the individual consumer and society as a whole through our design and innovation practices?

In summary, to have a corporate social mind, leaders must be willing to design product innovations with society at their core and be mindful of them throughout every process. The decisions made by companies and leadership with corporate social minds intentionally put society and societal benefit at the table every time, all the time. Creation of new products, services, and goods with the help of experts from relevant communities makes for longer-lasting and more impactful decisions that will lead to greater success for both shareholders and society's stakeholders. Remember to ask before deciding: In which ways does this decision affect the company, people, society, and the environment?

INTERVIEW

Rüdiger Fox,
Sympatex Technologies GmbH

"Today, we privatize profit and socialize the collateral damage . . . Sustainability needs to be radical."

RÜDIGER FOX, CEO of Sympatex Technologies GmbH, shares how he and his team made bold decisions to put environmental sustainability first in a market where many thought it was impossible. In this instance, Rüdiger implemented social-good changes even while the company was in "a financially critical situation." His interview shows how the company first examined its role in the ecological system surrounding its product, and then built its social-good efforts from there.

Michael: What does Sympatex do?

Rüdiger: People who spend a lot of time outdoors need clothing and shoes that keep them dry while controlling their body temperature in all types of weather. As a leading provider of sustainable functional textiles, Sympatex developed a special membrane that goes in between laminated textile layers that's 100% waterproof, 100% windproof, and breathable. It's our core product.

Michael: What is your role at Sympatex, and how do you engage with its social and environmental impact?

Rüdiger: Officially, my title is CEO. I'm not sure how other people view that title, but I think one of my most important roles is to provide a safe space for people to contribute to the purpose of the organization as much as they desire to—a space where they can grow and find the niches where they can contribute best.

My other important job is to understand the role the company has in the social or ecological system and to define our purpose in that context.

Michael: How would you describe the purpose of Sympatex?

Rüdiger: When I joined Sympatex three years ago, we sat down with all our employees and asked that question. The company was in a financially critical situation, and sometimes that allows you to go deep into fundamental questions. My questions were, "What is our reason for being? Does the world need us? If the world needs us, how we can define our role in a way that we can increase our impact?"

We came up with the definition of our core product. We're a bit more than 30 years old, and the core product has always possessed all the features of a closed-loop textile industry. So it turned out that we have actually had what we needed for 30 years to change the textile industry and make a significant impact on the environment.

And that became our purpose. We tabled any financial questions and agreed that the purpose of all our activity would be to accelerate the journey to making the functional textile industry a closed ecological loop and fully sustainable.

Michael: Can you expand on the company's social impact and its sustainability market?

Rüdiger: The textile industry basically causes negative social and environmental issues, and Sympatex's leverage is strongest on the environmental side. So that's where we focus. Product strategy, everything we're doing, is aimed at demonstrating how our industry—one of the dirtiest of the world—can become one of the cleanest with already available technology.

Externally, then, our strategic focus looks at sustainability. Internally, we rank the social side very high. We became a certified benefit corporation (known as a B Corp) so that we would be measured by that criteria. We also try to provide a work environment that's extremely trusting and joyful, if I may say so. Each employee can freely decide their own preferred number of working hours in a given week. Calling and emailing during vacations is strictly forbidden. When there's too much traffic or it's too hot or too cold to go out, then we want employees to work from home. We adjust the organization around the needs of our people.

In summary, we have this high social impact inbound and high environmental impact outbound. We know this isn't everything that needs to be done in the world, but we're trying to devote our energies where we have the best leverage.

Michael: How is the sustainability work connected to the company's innovation capabilities?

Rüdiger: I love that question! In many companies striving for both innovation and sustainability, someone comes up with an idea but doesn't have a way to close the loop, and the energy and enthusiasm the idea inspires just evaporates in a big space of random possibilities.

At Sympatex, we channel the ideas and possibilities in a certain direction so that every team member knows what we're aiming to accomplish. The speed of innovation we create in that direction then becomes enormous, especially for a company our size. Because everyone is working in the same direction, sustainability strategy has become one of the core elements of innovation for us.

> *"I was a convinced sustainability guy, because I just believe that when we see the impact of what we are doing and the resources we are burning, it's easy to understand it cannot go forever."*

Michael: Can you recall any specific moments at Sympatex when it was clear that complete sustainability really needed to be the driving force of the company?

Rüdiger: The one specific moment was the 24 hours when I was allowed to think about whether I would accept the job or not. I was a convinced sustainability guy, because I just believe that when we see the impact of what we are doing and the resources we are burning, it's easy to understand it cannot go forever. We're reaching limits, there's just no question. And if you reach limits, you need to find something new.

So, the first moment was looking at a company that had an amazing product at its core, yet had not achieved a relevant market share and had the lousiest sustainability balance sheet you could imagine. That's when I said wow, there's a great market—and we had a huge improvement potential. I couldn't find a better lab condition to test my theory that sustainability is the next "blue ocean" (a very open market).

The next moment was a few weeks ago, which was three years down the road. We had an internal leadership discussion, an honest one, asking how each of my first-level staff understood the purpose of the company. Nine out of 10 said profit—with the help of sustainability. Only one person said we improve the world and hopefully profit would come out of it. He was the only one who got it. I realized that even though you talk about taking sustainability into your core and have people live it for three years—they can still carry the old mental models in their heads.

So I hope that the third moment will be in another year or two, when everyone really gets it: We're about unconditional core sustainability with the hope that profit will follow.

Michael: Do you combine your environmental work with any social impact?

Rüdiger: Very rarely and only coincidentally. Because I think when you look at the system impact, yes, there are relationships, but they're not necessarily conditional. I try to make things simple. We create a small kids' book every year that we give as a free gift with kids' shoes that explains our story as simply as possible. We take one subject at a time—climate change and global warming, chemistry, plastic.

Michael: How would you describe the effect that environmental sustainability work has on your employees? Is it different from other companies you've worked for?

Rüdiger: I think the main difference is that we put CSR (corporate social responsibility) in the first rank of priorities, which is a radical shift from companies that just add it on. Now, annual financial results are part of overall results—but sustainability is the goal.

I saw a lot of skepticism to the craziness of this approach. During the economic upturn the company has seen over the last three years, it gradually changed into curiosity, and now it's starting to become trust. It's not yet fully there, because the world we live in believes that economics is driven by numbers.

Michael: How should companies tackle sustainability and community relations?

Rüdiger: I believe the world economy, especially in developed countries, operates on the approach of efficiency: more efficiency is better, faster efficiency is better; it's the idea of continuous improvement. But what we need to realize is that the world's resources can only take so much.

Sustainability and community relations—people relations—has a double effect. On one side, we are reaching the limit of the previous business model. On the other side, sustainability and the need of social improvement, justice, etc., will come so fast that it will change the economic system conditions overnight.

> *"Nobody will win in the end; we will just eliminate each other."*

For instance, once we face that global warming is real, CO_2 taxes will be introduced overnight, and if companies are not prepared, they will fail. If companies are prepared, and they are few, they will see what is called the "blue ocean." The "red ocean" is the economic model we have followed until now. Nobody will win in the end; we will just eliminate each other. Sustainability, mind you, is a positive opportunity of differentiation, of future efficiency. Today, we privatize profit and socialize the collateral damage. Once this society realizes that the collateral damage is too big and we are at that threshold, society and governments will push the responsibility back onto the industries.

If you understand that sustainability and social impact is a business opportunity and not a business constraint, you create a completely new business model. Sustainability needs to be radical. Sustainability is not a decoration, but it's the core space of business activity.

Michael: What two things would you tell a person who is about to design a new sustainability initiative for their company?

Rüdiger: Three things. First, realize that at the beginning, you'll be alone. You'll need pretty big shoulders, so if you don't have the daring to risk everything to stand up for your conviction, you'd better not start.

Second, if you're prepared to run the risk, then do it radically enough—not as an antithesis to the current business model, but as the next upgrade. We have made the mistake in the past of describing sustainability as a need to constrain, and this kind of language has given business the impression that sustainability will slow them down, creating enemy relations. That's unnecessary. Business talks mainly about optimization, not necessarily outcome, while sustainability criticizes the outcome. With a good optimization process that includes sustainability, you can affect the outcome.

Third, if the company makes the decision to go for it, do it full scale. If it's a compromise or a decoration, it won't work.

Michael: Were there any management principles or tools that helped you focus on these issues?

Rüdiger: Employee motivation, especially intrinsic motivation, was a core of my curiosity and personal learning. In business, we believe salary is the primary driver. What we need to realize is that fear and anxiety come from a place where, if one of 10 conditions isn't met, people will focus on the non-satisfied condition and not the nine you might have satisfied. Intrinsic motivation helps us understand humans much better—and not considering people in the company as a head count but as a bunch of creative individuals.

Michael: If you had to sum everything up, what would be the one most important argument for engaging in an environmental social issue?

Rüdiger: If you don't prepare today, tomorrow you will be eliminated. In just a handful of years, the pressure from environmental issues on any business will be big, and the companies that have prepared will stay and sustain. Those who waited will disappear.

CHAPTER 2

Trait 2: A Corporate Social Mind
Lives Its Values

A company's values set forth every employee's commit-ment to caring for their community and working toward an improved world. In an organization with a corporate social mind, employees at all levels consider social good as a vital part of their employer's existence, and they practice these values in their daily work.

The corporate social mind isn't only for external audiences. In fact, employees who believe in the social issues the company is embracing are vital to its authenticity and success. Engaged employees will ask the tough questions, go the extra mile, and be the advocates you need to advance toward actual social change.

Moreover, employees will be the first to notice—and call out—executives and employers (or former employers) who don't live up to their promises.

FOCUS

In this chapter, we will focus on how a company uses its values and connected beliefs to engage the public and partners in social-issue and community engagement programs. Specifically, we will address the following questions:

- Have we established internal or external values?
- Do our values represent and support society?
- How do we enact our values within product development and innovations?

TRAIT 2 IN ACTION

Much has been written about corporate values in general. Traditionally, value statements and beliefs express a company's position on how it operates and defines the manner in which all individuals and entities, both internal and external, perform their work and treat one another during the course of business.

These values tend to be operational values, rather than societal values.

In reviewing your own company values and beliefs, you must first determine if the company has adequately created corporate *societal* values—or, as we reference them in this book, corporate *social* values—that address the people, places, and issues impacted by the company.

No one can support your corporate social values if they don't know what you believe about people and society. If you do not anchor your identified social issues to beliefs that are accepted and practiced within and around your company's ethos, then you won't be able to effectively address those issues, be vocal about relevant policy, or design initiatives to support communities where your employees live, work, and play.

Any company committed to positive social change stands for something—and it has to be something that your like-minded employees, vendors, and partners will respond to and support during the course of business.

When crafting a belief statement, start with "We believe . . ." and then follow with a clear articulation of what your company stands for. For example:

> We believe that people who lack certain skills and knowledge can become successful by getting help from people who have succeeded and who are willing to commit their own time and resources to helping others achieve the same kind of success . . .

Or:

> We believe low-income neighborhoods hold tremendous untapped potential, and we work hard every day to connect consumers who believe the same to individuals who are desperate for a chance to prove themselves.

Or:

> We value the skills and talents of all people. We help our employees make a tangible difference in the lives of people who otherwise might not have the opportunity to show the world what they can do . . .

The point is to use language that shines a light on both sides of the equation.

Your company is the conduit between a community of consumers, activists, and change-makers who share and are passionate about your beliefs, causes, or issues. People (consumers and employees) are interested in what you believe; they want to know why you do what you do and who you are trying to help. Take pride in your work and the positive change you and your employees, partners, and vendors are helping to bring about.

Your corporate social values should require you to do several things: be present, be practiced, be supportive of society, and be authentic.

Be Present

Corporate social values must be present within the internal and external zeitgeist of the entity. This means those within your company must display, discuss, reference, and challenge one another openly in every action and performance of work to ensure society is considered in all decisions.

Be Practiced

The company must practice its corporate social values every day during the normal course of business. This means ensuring that corporate social values are referenced and practiced during product development, analysis of supply chain operations, and throughout marketing, sales, campaign efforts, and customer service.

Be Supportive of Society

Corporate social values must support society and not detract from societal interests, and they must be understood and practiced by employees every day. In a corporate social mind, how a company operates, manages its people, and stands for a better world are not mutually exclusive.

Be Authentic

Companies cannot tout corporate social values and then, when pressed to make critical decisions that affect the business and people, choose to ignore them in pursuit of personal gain/profit. The public will see and react to this inauthenticity, especially younger generations and consumers who seek authentic business operations and expect companies to live up to their values and beliefs. In essence, a company cannot stand up for issues, people, and communities in words and be weak in practice, and expect to get away with it without consequences.

Salesforce, Whole Foods Market, and American Express provide examples of social values within and among operational values.

SALESFORCE

Salesforce is an integrated customer relationship management solution that gives all a company's departments the same data on every customer. The company created salesforce.org as a social enterprise to reinvest revenue into communities, and it developed a number of programs aimed at youth education and workforce development.

Here are its core values:

- Trust
- Customer Success

- Growth

- Innovation

- Giving Back

- Equality for All

- Well-being

- Transparency

- Fun[1]

Marc Benioff, CEO and chairman of Salesforce, says it best: "You have the opportunity to set up companies that do good in the world. It's easy. There's all this incredible energy in your company, and you can unleash it for good. If you're not unleashing it, you're missing something."[2] Given this unique moment where public interest and consumer demands for companies to perform good work exists, leaders have more permission than ever before to create a corporate social mind.

WHOLE FOODS MARKET

Whole Foods calls itself America's Healthiest Grocery Store.™ The company emphasizes that its core values aren't situational, "but rather they are the underpinning of our company culture." Its core values follow:

- *We Satisfy and Delight Our Customers*—Our customers are the lifeblood of our business and our most important stakeholders. We strive to meet or exceed their expectations on every shopping experience.

- *We Promote Team Member Growth and Happiness*—Our success is dependent upon the collective energy, intelligence, and contributions of all of our team members.

- *We Care About Our Communities and the Environment*— We serve and support a local experience. The unique character of each store is a direct reflection of a community's people, culture, and cuisine.

- *We Practice Win-Win Partnerships with Our Suppliers*—We view our trade partners as allies in serving our stakeholders. We treat them with respect, fairness, and integrity, expecting the same in return.[3]

The relationships we have with everyone in the course of business create better outcomes for all. Looking far and wide at the company's role, decisions and relationships will ensure that social values transmit throughout the course of business and the end service and product.

AMERICAN EXPRESS

This financial services company believes that for people and businesses to thrive, they need strong communities.

Read on for American Express' core values.

- *Customer Commitment*—We develop relationships that make a positive difference in our customers' lives.

- *Quality*—We provide outstanding products and unsurpassed service that, together, delivers premium value to our customers.

- *Integrity*—We uphold the highest standards of integrity in all of our actions.

- *Teamwork*—We work together, across boundaries, to meet the needs of our customers and to help our company win.

- *Respect for People*—We value our people, encourage their development and reward their performance.

- *Good Citizenship*—We are good citizens in the communities in which we live and work.

- *A Will to Win*—We exhibit a strong will to win in the marketplace and in every aspect of our business.

- *Personal Accountability*—We are personally accountable for delivering on our commitments.

By creating "wins" that involve community and social issues along with business, the company takes a leading role and thus demonstrates its social values openly and authentically.[4]

CONNECTING CORPORATE SOCIAL VALUES TO YOUR WORK IN SOCIETY

To stand up for and live your corporate social values, you must help your consumers and the public at large understand how you consistently practice them.

In 2017, when US President Donald Trump issued an executive order banning Syrian refugees from entering the country, Levi Strauss' CEO Chip Bergh issued a strong response via a letter to his employees, part of which is quoted below:

Our country has benefited immensely from those who have come to the US to make a better life for themselves and their families, and we would not be the country we are today were it not for immigration. In fact, we would not be the company we are today if it weren't for Levi Strauss, who was himself an immigrant. He instilled a sense of doing what's right, and our company values of empathy, originality, integrity and courage are perhaps even more meaningful today than they were 163 years ago.

It's because of these values that we have never been afraid of diversity and inclusion or speaking up about it. We desegregated our factories in the US 10 years before it became the law of the land. We were one of the first companies to offer domestic partner healthcare benefits, long before it was popular. We have been a strong voice for inclusion, diversity and giving everyone an opportunity to achieve their fullest potential at LS&Co. regardless of race, gender, sexual orientation, nationality or religious preference. We know, deep in our soul, that diversity of all kinds is good for business and that a diverse organization will outperform a homogeneous one every time.

It is, in fact, our values that are guiding our perspective with respect to the executive order on immigration. Any policy that seeks to restrict or limit immigration based on race, nationality or religion is antithetical to what we believe as a company. Our success has been based on our ability to attract and retain the very best talent from all backgrounds, to embrace diversity, to be inclusive and benefit from different perspectives. Restricting the flow of talented individuals will, over time, impact the competitiveness of the country and the companies based here in the US.

We will not sit idly by. Because our employees are our first priority, we are reaching out to any employee who may be

continued

directly affected. We will stand by our colleagues and their families and offer support to any employee or family member directly affected by the ban.

Looking back on the history of this company, we are not afraid to take a stand on important issues of our day, and I believe this is one of those moments. If we stay true to our values and support those who champion equality and justice while working with policymakers to ensure our voice is heard, I'm confident our business and our communities will be stronger as a result.

These words inspired and rallied Levi's employees and its partners, and strengthened its commitment to the causes it supports. The company created a $1 million Rapid Response Fund to support vulnerable immigrants, refugees, the transgender community, and ethnic and religious minorities impacted by political events and the environment. The Levi Strauss Foundation gained visibility for its 65 years of advancing human rights and the well-being of underserved people in places where Levi Strauss & Co. has a business presence.

Levi Strauss' corporate social values guided its decisions and grounded its approach in that moment. By connecting its values and beliefs to their decisions and helping the public understand why decisions and actions are taken, the company reinforced its role as a corporate social leader. With a corporate social mind, your company's decisions and actions—your grants, initiatives, public statements about policies, and daily interactions with consumers—are all positioned and anchored in your corporate social values.

INTEGRATING CORPORATE SOCIAL VALUES THROUGHOUT YOUR BUSINESS SUPPLY CHAIN

Laura Spence and Michael Bourlakis, in their 2009 article "Moving from Corporate Social Responsibility to Supply Chain Responsibility," said that every player in a supply chain, regardless of their position, has a "supply chain responsibility" to integrate and promote social responsibility. This idea takes supply chain management far beyond its typical economic, operational, and legal components and contexts. To have a corporate social mind in supply chain management, you must analyze and consistently review every link to ensure that a strong social value system is being practiced and is benefiting society at every step.

Spence and Bourlakis identified four conditions for the successful integration of social responsibility in supply chains:

- A chain-wide commitment to achieving social (and environmental) benefits.

- The legitimacy and possibility of all links in the chain to have a voice.

- A genuine partnership approach.

- The acknowledgment of different approaches to ethics by different organizational forms within the supply chain.

The key to success in such a supply chain is a corporate social mind that can make sure all participants (backed by committed leaders and employees) buy in to a common goal to achieve, maintain, and deliver on the promises inherent in the corporate social values.

I was invited to visit a company that many people view as having done all there is to do related to social issue engagement—and done it masterfully. From everything I'd heard, visiting their corporate headquarters would be a little surreal: Here's where excellent social engagement, standing up for underrepresented populations consistently, and holding government publicly accountable for intruding on people's rights (or even thinking about it) were the norm.

The most fascinating part about exploring the culture of this organization was how clearly their public support of social issues was transmitted throughout the company to their products, sales teams, and marketing units. Walking through their offices, I saw corporate values listed on the walls—not just big words on posters, but values with specific examples from throughout their history when they lived up to them. Images and photos, words, newspaper clippings, and employee descriptions of the times the company had used its platform to address a social issue (and how it made them feel) superbly communicated their corporate values.

From the worker in the cafeteria lunch line showing a colleague her buttons and pins that represent the values and issues she cares about to the executive team opening up their meetings on values and the work they're doing, this company clearly is aligned with and living their values internally. My biggest takeaway is that this isn't just something the company uses externally; it is something this company truly lives daily.

TRAIT 2:
Design and Innovation Questions

When your company is designing your corporate social values, ask yourself the following questions:

- What makes our company unique in society, and how does it improve individual success within families, communities, and the world at large?
- Why does our company exist in society, and how does that purpose impact people, places, and the planet?
- Who do we serve (demographically, geographically, and our target audiences) and what do we provide that is special or compelling that moves society forward for those in communities of focus or globally?
- How do our work, people, services, goods, and/or knowledge help people?
- How can we demonstrate the impact on a single member of the public that came as a result of our intellect, services, and goods? How is their life trajectory affected? Will they be able to contribute to the broader community in ways they couldn't before?
- How does society and the world benefit from the improved prospects of the people we serve?

Many companies hold retreats or all-day workshops to develop and then share their corporate values with employees. They may print them on posters and publish them on their websites. Some might even include them in vendor contracts. However, for too many, that's as far as they go. The words get lost in the business of everyday work. Having a corporate social mind means giving those values life: inculcating the values in everyone who has a relationship with the company and integrating them into every process and decision.

INTERVIEW

Stephan Kohorst, Dr. Ausbüttel & Co. GmbH

"We find a lot of [employees] who are intrinsically moti-
vated and passionate about what they do . . . [That] has
a huge impact on corporate culture."

STEPHAN KOHORST, director and owner of Dr. Ausbüttel & Co. GmbH, shows how values guide his healthcare company in innovating products for patients and getting active in the community where employees work and live. You will notice the high percentage of employees and contractors who have some sort of disability, which makes the company's social issues even more relevant.

Michael: Can you describe your role at Ausbüttel and how you engage with social impact work there?

Stephan: I'm driven by intellectual curiosity and an entrepreneurial mindset. At Ausbüttel, we did a very, very detailed and profound value process with the management team and with all the staff to identify our company values—and the five we came up with are pretty much my personal values.

Freedom is a core value—the freedom for trial and error, to be creative.

The next one is trust—trusting yourself, which requires a certain self-confidence, but also means a tolerance for ambiguity, because quite often you can't control social projects and entrepreneurial projects.

The third value is performance—to really achieve something, to gain market share, to beat the big guys. Better than mediocracy or complacency.

The fourth one is an orientation—toward solutions and getting things done. Academics quite often over-theorize, and we Germans can be so fixated on getting into the problem that we forget we actually want to solve it.

The fifth value, and I think it's connected to all the other four, is social engagement—making a difference. I realized over time there's a strong connection between the two kinds of entrepreneurs I like most: a family entrepreneur and a social entrepreneur. The type I don't like is the social bureaucrat or shareholder focused on just financial value in the corporate sector, which I consider like a cancer on the market economy.

Michael: What is the focus of your company when it comes to social impact and sustainability?

Stephan: Theoretically we have three target groups, but we do 90-something percent of our work for two of them. The first of these is disadvantaged young people. Our social foundation is set up to finance work for children, palliative care, troubled youth—some criminal offenders and even a small percentage of sexual offenders . . . which was very tough for me. We also finance social work for young street prostitutes. We do a lot of mentoring now with young people from disadvantaged areas because we think we can make a difference and change biographies.

The second group is people with disabilities. About 10% of our staff here in Dortmund, Germany, has some form of disability. We also give work to 1,100 people with disabilities in other organizations, and we use a lot of inclusive hotels, and services, such as catering and gardening, for example.

Michael: I know you have a little bit of a skepticism when it comes to sustainability, but is it something your company looks at?

Stephan: I'm very passionate about social sustainability, such as integrating disadvantaged people. We try to be ecologically sustainable, as well. We built our new building with solar panels, and we pump water into the earth—and that's how we heat the whole building. We collect ice under the building in the winter, and we use it to cool the building in the summer instead of air conditioning. But I'm more passionate about people than about nature.

Michael: How is your social impact work connected with your innovation capabilities as a company in the healthcare sector?

Stephan: We find a lot of people who are intrinsically motivated and passionate about what they do. It's not a job mentality. It's not, "You pay me, that's why I do it. " This attitude has a huge impact on corporate culture and on the quality of our human resource. It gives us great human capital.

"So we're willing to invest 15 years in a project that helps children."

When it comes to product development . . . Six weeks ago, we launched a product for a rare disease that afflicts children and creates probably the toughest wound to heal. It's called EB, epidermolysis bullosa. Ten years ago, that product was our moonshot. It was way beyond our capabilities. When I said, "Look, we need to do something. This is a very painful change of wound dressings," we decided to invest a lot of time, money, and human resources toward creating a product that would lessen children's pain. Now that we've launched one, our objective is to spend the next five years finding a lot of patients to provide this product to, and then stop losing money on it. So we're willing to invest 15 years in a project that helps children.

It also has an impact on people here at the company. When they heard about it, when they saw the difference in feedback from patients, our people were really proud. Now we're thinking about the possibilities with palliative care, oncology, and horrible wounds and asking what we can do. We cannot heal a cancer patient, but we can offer more than consolation. We can create a huge impact on people's quality of life.

Michael: Was there any specific moment, personally or professionally, where you said, "This is the way we need to run this," by bringing the social into it?

Stephan: When I was 15 to 18, I spent a lot of time with a priest working in a prison. I was very impressed with what he had done, but I knew I wasn't courageous enough to live like him, and I wouldn't be a great social worker. So I became an entrepreneur and found these groups to help over time.

Michael: Can you describe a social impact initiative that you're especially proud of?

Stephan: I think our high level of inclusivity in our workforce is where we're unique. And regardless of their disability, we challenge them because we know they can do it. We treat every team member just like every other member of the team.

Across our entire staff, I think we have an extremely high proportion of intrinsically motivated people here. During a visit home to Poland, one woman working in research and development went to see an EB patient to better understand what we're doing here. When she came back, she told me I didn't need to motivate her anymore. Another nice story is about a woman who used to clean for us. She was an immigrant to Germany, and even though her background and academic training were considerable, she took the cleaning job because she needed to earn her living. She eventually told me about her background and academic training in Eastern Europe, and today she runs our research labs. These women and others like them don't care so much about incentives or a fancy office. They have a different value set.

Michael: How would you advise other companies to tackle social issues? Are there one or two steps you think are important?

Stephan: Allow for trial and error. Start small and don't make too many plans. Just do something, you know? Be hands-on, as an entrepreneur or a manager or whatever is your role, to gain the personal experience.

And don't do your social good just to look good or for human resource marketing. Once people begin to develop a cynical attitude toward corporate social responsibility, you will be worse off than if you never started. Be honest. Doing social impact work is not completely selfless or altruistic. Hey, it's a kick if you can enable other people, if you make things happen. The other thing you need to face is that there's going to be failure and ingratitude.

"And don't do your social good just to look good or for human resource marketing. Once people begin to develop a cynical attitude toward corporate social responsibility, you will be worse off than if you never started."

That's going to happen. That's life. So you will be disappointed. But then it comes down to, "Is it really important to you or not?" If it's important to you, you survive this kind of a disappointment and keep going forward.

CHAPTER 3

Trait 3: A Corporate Social Mind
Uses Resources for Society's Benefit

The SchlaU-Schule in Munich is a vibrant place of human destiny. On a normal day, young people from all around the world are entering and leaving the school discussing their homework, an upcoming exam, their next internship, or just the events of the last barbecue. A beehive's activity pales in comparison to this center of excellence in education. The 320 students who attend the school all came to Germany as unaccompanied minor refugees. In less legalistic terms, this means they were 18 or younger and arrived without parents or relatives.

The stories these youngsters tell are heartbreaking, sometimes horrific—but are all told with a sense of hope and feeling at home in this school. The school has won an endless list of prizes for its work, not only in the field of integration and refugee work, but also as an educational institution; 98% of the students graduate every year. The people who made the school possible, especially its founder, Michael Stenger, are risk-takers, visionaries, pragmatists, and professionals in their various fields.[1]

You might ask why this story about a school is in a book on the corporate social mind. Because companies contributed and continue to contribute to the success of this organization. They do so way beyond the obvious financial donations as you can see below:

- Hilti, a global developer and manufacturer of tools for the construction, facility management, and manufacturing industry, supports the school with its resources and networks in the construction industry. The school has repeatedly had to move to new locations, and Hilti supported them with building design, planning, and even hands-on rebuilding by employees and customers.

- Springer Nature, a global science publishing house, advised the organization on knowledge management and book production when the school wanted to turn its curricula and experience with unaccompanied minor refugees into a book for teachers, public administrators, and educational nonprofits.

- goetzpartners, a management consultancy, has been a strategic advisor to the organization for many years. Its partners and consultants have provided coaching for staff, supported the development of a business plan, and identified new financing and fundraising strategies. The German business weekly *WirtschaftsWoche* honored goetzpartners with the Best Pro Bono Project 2018 award for its long-term work with the school.

- Several Munich-based companies have encouraged their employees to become mentors for the students of the school. These mentorships often go far beyond a corporate volunteering program, requiring time commitments well beyond what companies normally allow employees for social engagement.

Most of these companies have also supported the SchlaU-Schule with a donation, either directly or through a corporate foundation. Their real pride, however, comes from their unique contributions of time, skills, knowledge, and networks.

FOCUS

Using resources for society's benefit means companies use their intellectual, social, financial, and emotional capital to drive ideas that advance progress in society.

In this chapter, we will navigate and explore answers to the following questions:

- What resources can companies mobilize for society's benefit?
- Why do companies often start out with giving money and then begin to invest a variety of resources?
- What is corporate volunteering? What are some categories of this form of engagement?
- Why are your employees such an important component of the corporate social mind?

Companies have many resources through which they can express their corporate social mind. It is important to note that these resources can be mobilized as part of the core business, or they can be part of community engagement that's expressed through marketing, communications, and external social impact work.

TRAIT 3 IN ACTION

Companies can use various types of resources in a corporate social mindset. These resources can be categorized as capital via the **FIITTTS Model**:

Financial
In-kind
Intellectual
Time
Transmission
Trust
Social

The FIITTTS Model is an easy way for your team to define a holistic approach to addressing social issues through innovation and resource modeling. Let's explore the FIITTTS model in more depth.

Financial Capital

A company can invest in a new product or a start-up that contributes to solving a societal challenge. It can make a loan to a community organization or donate to a not-for-profit organization.

- French food company Danone has created an ecosystem of social investment funds. Its Livelihoods Fund for Family Farming or the Livelihoods Carbon Funds provide financial resources for a variety of start-ups and other ventures trying to solve specific challenges around food production, climate change, family farming, and food distribution.

- Salesforce has made donations to organizations around the world that actively provide measures against youth unemployment. The support is part of the software company's 1% pledge to commit resources, such as products and time, to "improving the state of the world."[2] It may not be a surprise that the SchlaU-Schule in Munich is one of the organizations the company has supported.

- MAC Cosmetics donates all profits from its VIVA GLAM lipstick line to raise attention and funds for the fight against HIV/AIDS. The company was an early mover in this cause when it realized how the pandemic affected the fashion and other creative industries. The MAC AIDS Fund has become an important, respected, and knowledgeable global funder for this cause.

When you think about your company's financial capital related to social good, the following questions can help you thoroughly consider your approach:

- What impact do we want to achieve?

- How much money do we want to invest in societal issues?

- Do we just want to give grants or also give loans to and even invest in the equity of social start-ups?

- What funding periods do we want to commit to?

- Do we give on our own or together with others?

- Do we want to raise funds for a cause through one of our products?

In-kind Capital

Besides money, time, and expertise, a company's products can also help ameliorate a societal problem. In retail and similar industries, donations of space can help solve a challenge.

It is common practice today for supermarkets and food companies to work together with food banks. They pass on surplus goods to these not-for-profit organizations for distribution or food preparation to benefit the community. Many software companies provide their products to the not-for-profit sector for free or at reduced rates.

Donating products requires you to consider a new category of questions. If you determine your product could support a cause, think about whether the transaction makes sense for you and for the nonprofit:

- Can they store and distribute the product?

- What are the delivery costs?

- What liability, tax, and intellectual property questions do we need to answer before making the gift?

- Do we want to publicize this kind of giving? If yes, how?

Intellectual Capital

Companies have such a wealth of talent (people), knowledge, and skills that it can mobilize for society. They can use their talent to drive social innovation, help a community organization with its accounting or business plan, develop an awareness campaign for an issue—or help clean up a beach.

For example, logistics companies around the world regularly share their knowledge, skills, and equipment with not-for-profit organizations and governments in the wake of natural disasters and humanitarian catastrophes.

Lawyers and law firms around the world provide pro bono services to not-for-profits, helping with contracts, employment issues, or specific legal cases. Some law firms have made providing a certain percentage of this kind of work to society a core ethos.

This type of giving can be invaluable to a cause that needs but can't afford to hire expertise. Look across all your departments and ask these questions:

- What kind of talent and knowledge do we have?

- How could these resources support the societal issues we have committed to?

- What workplace culture and human resource issues (i.e., time-off requests, approvals and response, dedicated support to fulfill) must we consider when our employees support community organizations?

Time Capital

Many companies today encourage their employees to volunteer and provide them with time off—often even paid—to do so. Employees may also be staffed on pro bono projects for not-for-profit organizations or social start-ups.

For example, companies around the world encourage their employees to mentor young people. Companies also organize volunteering days where together they clean up a park, paint a school, or organize a fundraiser—like a bake sale or lemonade stand—for a cause.

First, decide the basics:

- Do we want to encourage managers to give time off?

- Do we (or can we) provide our employees with paid time to commit to a cause?

- How does volunteering integrate into our employee engagement culture?

Then, consider an implementation plan that involves participation at every level within the organization. When managers participate, more employees do so, too.

A NOTE ABOUT CORPORATE VOLUNTEERING

Enlightened companies have always considered their employees as *the* crucial resource in business success. Around the world, they are increasingly doing so when it comes to their community and cause commitments, as well. The FIITTTS Model has already shown how important employees are to mobilizing assets.

"Corporate volunteering," the term often used for this form of engagement, has become an indicator in a variety of sustainability ratings. The Dow Jones Sustainability Index, for instance, asks companies for their employees' volunteering hours. You can argue whether such a quantitative indicator can say a lot about the quality of a company's social commitment, but the indicator has raised awareness of this asset for society.

Corporate volunteering these days is especially relevant to employee engagement. The emotional commitment of an employee to a company and its goals is a revealing indicator for employee retention and productivity. The millennial generation, especially, connects employee engagement with a company's societal/environmental engagement—its corporate social mind.

Companies also use corporate volunteering for leadership development and even include it in HR assessment schemes. Many companies these days provide team interventions in which high-potential managers work with an NGO to solve a problem for the latter. Other companies facilitate employee sabbaticals in NGOs. The options seem to be endless.

In the past, research has differentiated the following two forms of corporate volunteering:

continued

Skills-based volunteering: Employees engage in volunteering activities that utilize their specific professional skills and expertise.

Traditional volunteering: Employees engage in volunteering activities that do not require them to utilize their specific professional skills and expertise.[3]

While these forms of volunteering seem aligned with intellectual and time resources as described in the FIITTTS Model, we must be aware of another form of valuing employees: recognizing their own personal community engagement and matching their personal cause donations. Matching employee donations is now a common practice, especially since a variety of software tools make this process easy to administer. The foundation for the German railway service Deutsche Bahn, for instance, does this with its "Ehrensache"—points of honor—award, annually acknowledging extraordinary employee civic engagement with public recognition and a donation.

Corporate volunteering has become a steady offering in the world of business and, done properly, can be an amazing tool for motivating employees while supporting a social cause. As you have seen, many companies have integrated corporate volunteering into various dimensions of management, especially human resources and corporate culture. There's one caveat to this: Managers must remember (or be reminded) that the essence of corporate volunteering is "voluntary," something an employee does without pressure because of an intrinsic motivation.

A corporate social mind is a holistic start for bringing your employees on board for contributing to the community through the many resources your company has at hand. Through you, organizations like the SchlaU-Schule can thrive and do amazing things for young people and our society.

Transmission Capital

A company has a variety of options it can employ for communicating about a cause (see chapter 5 on having a social voice): public relations, marketing channels, and other communication measures.

For example, over the last few years, companies in France (OneInThreeWomen), Germany (The Chefsache Initiative), or the UK (Business Fights Poverty) have worked together to communicate their strong belief in the importance of diversity and social cohesion. Various brand campaigns have taken a stance on societal issues ranging from gender perception, like H&M's "She Is a Lady," to climate change, like true fruits' "Say Yes to Plastic," to homelessness, like Fritz-Kola's "#nursoamrande." On environmental issues, retailers like Carrefour (France), REWE (Germany), Hofer (Austria), Sainsbury's (UK), and Patagonia and Starbucks (US), and members of the food industry, like Ricola (Switzerland), sweetgreen (USA), and Ritter SPORT (Germany) have actively campaigned together with nonprofit organizations to promote the protection of bees and other ecological causes.

Communicating to your audiences about your social issues and your particular causes isn't so different from how you communicate to consumers about any particular product. Consider these common targeting questions:

- What marketing and communications means do we have?

- What channels can we use as part of our societal engagement?

- Depending on our business (B2C, B2B, etc.), who do we reach (audiences), and what is the appropriate way to address these target groups?

Trust Capital

Trust may be the hardest asset to grasp, yet it's the most important. Trust is about creating an emotional, empathetic relationship with your community—with society. If you want to embody a corporate social mind, you must develop trusting relationships with your partners in the community. You must absolutely be willing to accept other forms of professionalism in other sectors—and the fact that business logic may not work when trying to support a societal cause.

For example, even though a retail chain may have had grants solely to community partners in the past, it has been handed a close relationship with a healthy lifestyle education NGO and is prepared to enter into a five-year partnership. This new type of relationship will be based on the understanding that the issue at hand needs longer-term interventions, but more important, it is an expression of trust in the organization and its work.

These questions should spark some deep internal discussions:

- What is important for us in a trust relationship (transparency, human relations, etc.)?

- How can we use the trust that people have in management, employees, or our brands to leverage commitment to a cause?

Social Capital

Social capital is a widely used term in the social sciences, but it is often hard to grasp. We focus on a company's relationships and the values partners and networks can create for social good.

As a company, you and your employees have many ties to local, regional, national, and global communities—networks that often are an important part of your business success. But these networks can now also become part of how you drive social change as you partner with other entities from various sectors of the community.

For example, a manufacturing company connects the homeless NGO it supports with the accounting firm it uses; in turn, the latter offers pro bono services to the NGO. In another, the CEO of a service provider connects a company-supported environmental NGO with an education NGO so the two NGOs can develop a joint program. In a third, a company convenes all stakeholders in the community at a production site to talk about improving secondary education (see chapter 6 on social collectives).

Think hard and do some digging when answering these questions about your own relationships:

- What does our company's extended network look like (have you ever mapped it?)?

- Who are we in touch with regularly?

- What new partnerships among these players could we potentially create?

- What compliance measures need to be addressed when connecting suppliers, customers, etc., around a community issue?

As you have seen, the FIITTTS Model is an easy way to get an initial understanding of your resources and how you can mobilize them as part of your community involvement. We aver that the FIITTTS Model plus a company's values proposition constitute the basic setup of a corporate social mind.

Realizing that companies have a variety of resources to use for social change can often come as an epiphany. It's crucial that companies considering their role in society recognize from the start that they have a lot more resources than they do funds. Money is important, of course, but it may not be the resource that will have the most impact for a cause.

This became clear during an extensive strategic review and development process for a large technology and engineering company's global corporate citizenship engagement. The company was slightly uneasy about its existing community impact and suspected that company-related activities around the world were not communicating the correct message about its desired engagement.

The company was right, and the differences were traced back to company resources.

In interviews with managers who oversaw corporate citizenship engagement at the company's sites in more than 30 countries—managers who worked in communications, executive offices, and human resources—we found that each manager determined which company resources to apply to social issues engagement. The company had no overarching plan or structure to guide these regional managers in implementing engagement within their own area's community and culture. Some sites let employees fundraise for local charities, while others offered the pro bono expertise of engineers on development projects. Some gave in-kind donations. The list of activities conducted (and resources used) seemed haphazard.

These discoveries helped us start a brand-new conversation with the company's headquarters about its goals for societal impact. In fact, management had been surprised by the many creative ways employees had found to engage with social causes, and so their discussions became laser-focused on how to leverage employees' enthusiasm and knowledge for social impact—and how to make these efforts known within the company.

This shift in management's mindset was a game changer for the company's strategic outlook. Management realized how much more it could do and how many new types of impact the company could have if it thought beyond a simple corporate financial donation. Today, the company approaches all corporate social responsibility (CSR) decisions by applying all its assets (human capital and intellectual resources) to the social issues they want to address.

The experience was a game changer for our advisory team, too, and we began to think of our own volunteering based more on our skills and our knowledge of things like software. This was the spark that began to shape the concept of a corporate social mindset.

Every day, managers think about resources for driving a business cause. With a corporate social mind, you also consider these resources for driving social-good engagement. It's a real joy (and often a quick win) to view your company through this lens. The great thing is that this mindset opens the door to one of the most basic ideas of business: In one way or another, the services provided and the products invented should make life better.

TRAIT 3:
Design and Innovation Questions

It takes all types of capital to put a corporate social mind into practice. To help ensure yours permeates your company, consider these three questions:

- What issues, based upon our employee and consumer interests, can we apply the FIITTTS model to?
- How do we capitalize on the resources out in the community and leverage our company's resources for the issue?
- How will we nudge our employees to utilize their talents and assets (time, financial resources, etc.) through the company for the issues of most importance?

Companies have so much more than money to use to support a cause and advance societal change. The corporate social mind takes a hard look at its business to see what type of assistance it can best provide, whether that be employees building shelters, backpacks for school children, quarterly accounting reviews, management consultations, or something else (the sky's the limit). Then, the team can figure out how to deliver such assistance most effectively. Today's consumers, employees, and policymakers expect corporate social issue engagement, and the corporate social mind is best positioned to meet these expectations.

INTERVIEW

Daniel Lee, Levi Strauss Foundation and Levi Strauss & Co.

"Critical to our approach and consistent with our being linked to a company with a 166-year legacy . . . is patience, which I think is a vastly underrated virtue in philanthropy."

AS EXECUTIVE DIRECTOR of the Levi Strauss Foundation, Daniel Lee stands on the shoulders of giants in the world of corporate social responsibility—like LS&Co. chairman emeritus and former CEO Bob Haas. This legacy gives him the permission to push the foundation to be bold in support of marginalized communities around the globe, even in the face of tension. Here, he discusses why Levi Strauss is in it for the long game.

Derrick: Please give us some background on your role at the Levi Strauss Foundation and Levi Strauss & Co.

Daniel: I'm executive director of the Levi Strauss Foundation, a role I've held for 11 years. Our charge is to take on the issues and events of our time and be an expression of our company's values—originality, empathy, integrity, and courage. We are the primary philanthropic arm of the company, aiming to drive long-term social change on the issues we care about. One thing that makes us distinctive among other corporate funders is that we tend to get in early and stay the course.

Over the course of decades, we have focused on three core areas: 1) the rights and well-being of the people who make our products, 2) ending the HIV/AIDS epidemic, and 3) social justice.

Critical to our approach, and part and parcel with being linked to a company with a 166-year track record of giving back to the community, is patience, which I think is a vastly underrated virtue in philanthropy—especially corporate philanthropy. In recent years, we've seen the tools of the business and consulting sectors barrel through the fields of philanthropy and corporate citizenship like freight trains, on the tracks of what I like to call "the gospel of innovation." No doubt, there are many positive aspects of innovation, but there are also unintended consequences and downsides. This gospel exalts what is new and disruptive over what is tried and true. Too often we see philanthropic or corporate citizenship initiatives with a shelf life of two or three years, and then it's on to the next new idea. We can't forge durable or meaningful social change without commitment, continuity, and consistency.

Derrick: In the book, we talk about patience and that it's a marathon, not a sprint. Can you share an example?

Daniel: In the early days of addressing the HIV/AIDS epidemic, we helped nonprofit organizations get off the ground with an issue no other sector was willing to support—first in the Bay Area and then across the globe. Over time, this portfolio evolved to focus on prevention work and then on advocacy work for the benefit of those who bear the brunt of the epidemic. We've stayed the course with $75 million in grants over almost four decades, pivoting along the way to changing realities and needs.

It's fitting to be agile, responsive, and creative in driving social change, but the trend we're seeing among funders to launch and then sunset programs at breakneck speed is a matter of concern: This is not only vain and ineffective; it is foolhardy.

Derrick: How do you maintain the company's values in everything you do?

Daniel: It's critical for every institution to have its own narrative, its own genealogy of why it does what it does. Our root story is Levi Strauss himself, who emigrated to the US from Germany while escaping religious persecution. At the height of the Gold Rush, he moved westward to San Francisco to open a dry goods business before partnering with a tailor named Jacob Davis to create the ultimate garment for workers, the blue jean.

> *"To me the litmus test is, are you willing to take a stand on the values that you care about? And do you have the courage to be the first—even in the face of tension or unpopularity?"*

He was viewed equally as a business leader and philanthropist, giving back to the people, institutions, and causes that he cared about. We look to his generosity, courageous risk-taking, and commitment to values as our legacy. A number of high-water marks in Levi Strauss & Co.'s citizenship history also serve as guiding stars. The company's factories in the American South were racially integrated even before it was mandated by law in 1964. It was the first company to implement a code of conduct with labor, social, and environmental standards for all contracted suppliers in 1991. It was the first company to provide domestic partner benefits to same-sex couples.

To me the litmus test is, are you willing to take a stand on the values that you care about? And do you have the courage to be first—even in the face of tension or unpopularity?

When Levi Strauss & Co. made the decision in 1992 to apply its non-discrimination policy and discontinue employee-matching gifts to the Boy Scouts of America, it received 130,000 letters—mostly negative—through a consumer campaign orchestrated by a conservative religious organization. But the company stood its ground. A *New York Times* article written a few years later captured the significance of this stand: " . . . Levi Strauss is taking a hard line on the new diversity of society." The article mentioned that it was unprecedented for a company to hold its ground in the face of this type of consumer boycott.[4]

Derrick: Let's talk about social justice. I know that both the foundation and the company have been involved for many years. Talk about where you see the work going forward.

Daniel: For the fourth consecutive year, the Levi Strauss Foundation is allocating $1 million to a Rapid Response Fund that supports organizations that protect the civil liberties of highly vulnerable communities across the United States and abroad—including immigrants, refugees, the transgender community, and religious minorities—who are facing a myriad of threats in this disruptive policy environment. On the heels of the last US Presidential election, our CEO, Chip Bergh, addressed employees. He said this is a moment to show the country and the world what it means to be a values-driven institution. I'm proud that Levi Strauss & Co. has used its voice and influence on the issues that we care about, whether standing alongside vulnerable immigrants,

standing beside Muslims, decrying the inhumane treatment of asylum seekers, and taking stands for LGBT inclusion. It's not merely
a rainstorm for the communities we have long cared about but a
sustained monsoon—and we've decided to enshrine this stream of
funding to protect the weak and vulnerable in society as a mainstay
of our philanthropic work.

> *"Are we organizing our society around the protection*
> *of those who are most vulnerable and putting them at*
> *the center of our project of democracy?"*

We've pivoted to name this portfolio the Strategic Response
Fund because many of our grantees are not only defending groups
in the immediate crosshairs of policy decisions and actions but also
are playing a long game in offense. Their efforts resonate powerfully
with an essence of the Levi's brand: We're at our strongest when
we're at the center of culture and helping define it.

We must ask the question: Are we organizing our society
around the protection of those who are most vulnerable and putting them at the center of our project of democracy? We know
the alternative—and that playbook is all about separating, segre-
gating, vilifying, and removing.

In moments of disruption, different voices come out of the
woodwork, different alliances happen, and I feel like our grantees and the foundation are helping the company live its values.
Likewise, the voice of our company is aligning in a way that is
part of a greater "we," alongside our longstanding partners in
ways that I think stand up to this moment and our legacy.

CHAPTER 4

Trait 4: A Corporate Social Mind Listens before Acting

C ompanies with a corporate social mind listen to society before driving innovation and implementation. Before taking any action or designing and executing new products, services, and solutions, these companies first listen in order to understand societal benefit, impact, and desires.

Listening to conversations that are already happening around your issue is imperative to understanding. Without real listening, companies run the risk of making decisions based only on impersonal data shared by experts and researchers. Such information has its place, but it cannot and should not replace hearing from the individuals who are directly and tangentially affected by your issue.

FOCUS

Listening is more important than talking—this is a general rule of life that also applies to companies that have a corporate social mind. In this chapter, we will help answer key questions on listening to consumers, community, and partners:

- How do we create opportunities for listening throughout the innovation process?
- How can we get consistent data on how our consumers and community respond to our actions?
- What listening opportunities should we create in an effort to understand the current dialogue about the social issues we desire to address?

TRAIT 4 IN ACTION

In neighborhoods identified as food deserts (local areas without fresh food markets), residents lack access to healthy food options due to reasons such as physical disabilities, lack of transportation, etc. The supermarket chain Kroger heard from such neighborhoods in Louisville, Kentucky. In 2017, more than 116,000 people living in Jefferson County (Louisville) didn't have reliable access to affordable healthy food.[1] These residents needed a grocery store that offered fresh food, including fruits and vegetables.

Kroger knew that opening stores in some of these communities just wasn't feasible, but from listening to the community and having conversations with neighborhood groups, the company designed a new approach to address the issue of food insecurity.

"It does not have to be a brick-and-mortar store for us to provide access to healthy food for people," said Erin Grant, a spokeswoman with Kroger's Louisville division, in the *Louisville Courier Journal*. "That might not always be the solution. There really are other ways."[2]

So, in partnership with a local food bank, Kroger created a mobile market, which actually brought healthier food directly to the most affected communities. The market puts fruits and vegetables in displays all over the place, including outside the mobile unit, in an effort to illustrate the fresh produce within the small market. More than 200 products line the shelves of the mobile market that has two refrigerated units containing fresh meat, dairy products, and eggs, to name some of the items. At the checkout station, customers' grocery bills automatically reflect the Kroger sale prices. The mobile market makes 35 stops at 29 low-income housing complexes, schools, parks, and community centers. The market serves 30 to 50 people at each location, with average sales between $500 and $1,000.[3]

In every successful venture by companies to design and encourage new innovations and social impact, it's clear that leaders have taken the time to listen first and create later. When you listen before you create, cultural, environmental, and social influences rally to your cause and encourage consumers and the public to engage with you on your customer journey. The same holds true for social issues. Response to social issues doesn't come solely from wonderful communication and marketing efforts backed by amazing new innovations. It comes because companies create opportunities that take into account the specific cultural, social, and environmental circumstances and leverage these elements to make social impact happen.

The purpose of listening, especially within the context of the corporate social mind, is to learn and adapt to meet and exceed expectations by stakeholders, shareholders, and the community by providing what the affected audience truly needs. Specifically, this means:

- The company with ears and eyes in the community they serve (and ultimately want to impact) understands the appropriate approach better than those who seek to perform social change without engaging the audience it will impact.

- The individuals you involve feel that their voice is being heard rather than ignored in the approach to social change.

- In terms of risk management, companies listen to employee perspectives on how work can be accomplished more efficiently, effectively, and safely.

- The process of listening forms bonds with stakeholders (social capital) vital to existing and future social impact initiatives.

WE MUST LISTEN TO EVERYONE

Mariana Gomes, the co-founder of MUB Cargo, has defined three perspectives to take into account when trying to understand what consumers and the public really want: internal perspective, data perspective, and outside perspective. We can adapt these to our corporate social mind approach to listening by considering the following questions:

Corporate Social Listening Approach Perspectives

INTERNAL PERSPECTIVE

- What do our internal teams think about our product or service and why consumers use it?

- Social Mindset Adaptation: What do our internal teams think are the most important issues we should address in our communities with our expertise, and what is informing this response/reaction?

DATA PERSPECTIVE

- What data do we already have on our consumers, and what does it tell us?

- Social Mindset Adaptation: What do we know about current consumers and the social, cultural, and environmental conditions that influence their behaviors?

OUTSIDE PERSPECTIVE

- What do our consumers, partners, suppliers, and any other external entities tell us about our product or service?

- Social Mindset Adaptation: What do our consumer, community stakeholders, local residents, and partners tell us about the current issues affecting them?

Each of these perspectives helps corporate leaders understand the dynamics and influences that communities and consumers have on one another. Together, they give the company a finger on the pulse of consumers and allow society to be at the heart of all decisions, which directly impacts opportunities for product and service innovations.

Two companies that have exercised this approach of listening and then engaging in social issues are Proctor & Gamble (P&G) and yogurt brand Yoplait. Both companies entered into conversations on social issues deliberately and cautiously by listening first.

- *P&G*—In the "We See Equal" ad campaign, P&G took on the issue of gender bias. The multichannel campaign depicted boys and girls defying gender stereotypes. Because discussions about gender and gender equality were particularly heightened during the US general election of 2016, P&G needed to ensure it was not perceived as jumping on the politically charged bandwagon, so it ran the ads after the election. The company was well aware from its own internal and external research that this was the right move. With 45% female managers and 33% female board members, P&G could easily demonstrate its own dedication to equality in the workplace. This action by a business pushing for social change was seen as authentic and was well received by consumers and the public.

- *Yoplait*—To engage mothers, Yoplait decided to enter the so-called mom-shaming debates—the often preachy or patronizing information aimed at mothers about how to be a good mother and shaming those who don't fit the mold. In a campaign titled "Mom On," Yoplait invited mothers to address being judged on issues of breastfeeding, working, and consuming alcohol. The campaign did not take a particular stance; it simply recognized that shaming conversations exist. For Yoplait, the decision was a good one, ultimately connecting and reconnecting the brand with its core audience of mothers. According to analysis from Google, the ads resulted in a 1,461% increase in brand interest.[4]

Listening Approaches

If you are a leader in marketing or social impact at your company, you have a frontline opportunity to perform listening market research to deeply understand consumer and public interests, sentiments, and environmental conditions regarding social issues. If your company already performs consumer insight research, now is the time to seek additional data on your social issue interests and consumers' pro-social behaviors by deploying any of the approaches below:

- **Formal Research**

Conduct qualitative (focus groups, consumer and public panels, individual interviews), quantitative (surveys), and social listening analysis to measure the company's impact on consumers and society.

- **Feedback Loops**

Create regular feedback loops that go beyond purchasing behaviors in order to see (from the consumer's vantage point) how consumption takes place for them, given their particular situations.

- **Observation/Listening**

Participate in events, social opportunities, and in-home exercises so that you can hear or observe firsthand the diverse perspectives of individual consumers within target audiences about the company's community involvement and approaches to social issues.

In addition, consider utilizing key tactics to ensure ongoing efforts to understand the effects of social issues on the public, including your consumers:

- Consistently have a finger on the pulse of issues affecting consumers, partners, and communities where the company conducts business. This means creating ongoing mechanisms for data and observation to proactively address potential issues related to innovations, product development, and social issue engagement.

- Deliberately plan stakeholder conversations, feedback sessions, and input collection. A proactive schedule of interactions will set your company up for ongoing, responsive, and longer-term dialogue.

- Include various stakeholders, consumers, and employees in listening sessions, and ensure your exercises are created with diversity in mind. Every person brings inherent biases to conversations, surveys, etc., so you must be aware of other viewpoints.

- Consider conducting an ongoing/recurring survey or attending/observing an event at key convenings of

the social issue you address or where it will be dis-
cussed. The key at this point is to be present, but not
contribute. Spend time listening instead of sharing.

- Apply consistent listening and feedback tools digitally
and in person. So many new methods are available
for listening and research. Include digital approaches
(online interviews, focus groups, etc.); if resources are
limited, supplement with in-person observation and
focus groups or personal interviews.

- Report insights garnered from listening and observing the impact of social issue initiatives and prod-
ucts/services to the public regularly. Help the public
understand what milestones you achieved and the
next milestone you are using all your assets to reach.
Helping others understand what you are doing and
what you are focused on is an easy way to bring in
partners to join your efforts.

Your organization already may be monitoring social media and
conducting regular surveys. But as you'll see from the following
story, that's not the same as *listening*.

HEARING IS NOT LISTENING

After finishing a kickoff meeting with a new corporate client seeking to address gun violence, we asked them if we could take them
on a field trip different from any they were used to going on.

By way of background, the company had already gone out of
its way to bring in issue experts, journalists who covered the issue

for outlets across the country, and field researchers who had led wonderfully designed studies using methods we would have recommended. Company executives proudly told me, "We feel like we know enough because of the listening tour we just finished."

From their perspective, they had done everything necessary to create a sound, solid strategy. However, while they had learned much from the experts they surrounded themselves with, neither the marketing team nor the internal social impact department staff had ever talked one-on-one with a person who was actually impacted by the issue. Their listening tour had consisted of people talking *about* the issue, but no one in the company had gained the social, cultural, and environmental perspectives needed to truly understand how the issue affected people's daily lives.

The result was that their executives could rattle off statistics, but they were at a loss when it came to writing an effective message about the audience. This is not an uncommon occurrence. In this era of technology and information overload, it's easy to get knowledge about an issue. But to truly understand attitudes and behaviors, we have to use a more traditional way of gathering information: We have to get firsthand accounts from those involved.

In contrast to the "listening tour" the company had taken, the field trip we planned was to visit three families affected by the issue the company wanted to address. Marketers heard firsthand accounts from people in their homes, observing each person— including facial gestures and body language—as they talked. This allowed them to truly understand and humanize the data they heard about on their listening tour. The result, this time, was the ability to tell emotion-based stories and make decisions that were grounded in authentic, human information.

TRAIT 4:
Design and Innovation Questions

Consider asking the following questions as you design opportunities to gather data and insights on your consumers' and the public's engagement regarding social issues:

- How will we embed listening about social issues and the individual's environmental conditions into innovation and production development?
- What approach can we use to provide consistent insights on the social issues affecting consumers and our target audience(s)?
- How will our internal and external stakeholders use the data in their work?

As you design and iterate your approaches to social issues (and you will iterate as your consumers and the public engage in issues in real time), remember to listen all the way: Embed yourself in the affected community. Understand the correlations and relationship your consumers have with the issue. This not only makes good business sense but creates a corporate social mindset.

INTERVIEW

Christine Montenegro McGrath,
Mondelēz International

"It's all of us—farmers, producers, consumers—winning together. That doesn't just mean Mars and Nestlé and Hershey winning together with Mondelēz. It means the cocoa farmers having a livelihood and winning with us."

CHRISTINE MCGRATH, vice president and chief of global impact at Mondelēz International, shares how her company listened to cocoa farmers and created sustainable processes to benefit everyone in the supply chain. Notice how she moved the company from an "it's the right thing to do" philosophy to an "it's the right thing to do for our business" mentality.

Derrick: Please give us some background on yourself and your role at Mondelēz.

Christine: Sure. I've been with the company for 25-plus years, first on the Kraft and then the Mondelēz side. I've spent two-thirds of my career in a marketing and/or innovation role, trying to understand consumers' needs and how I could either evolve an existing brand or create a new one and then new products to meet evolving consumer needs.

I led teams that got really good at what we call white space innovation (looking at a problem or an opportunity we've never tackled before and maybe others in our industry haven't, or haven't as well as they could). That led to me leading sustainability and well-being, figuring out how we could better link our brands to our sustainability work.

> *"For a business to take an issue on and commit to making a difference, I think it has to be integral to its business."*

Kraft and Mondelēz became separate companies in 2012, and Mondelēz focused on global snacking. We studied consumers in China, Brazil, the UK, and the US, and we learned that well-being is very holistic for consumers. Not just, "What am I eating and putting into my body?" but also, "Where did the food come from? Who grew it? Who are the people behind and connected to it? What's it doing to the community where they come from? What's it doing to my local community?" People think about the ripple effect that food has on themselves and their environment, and they understand more and more the effects of the choices they make. They recognize that their choices influence what happens in the world.

Derrick: Did you experience any pushback early on? How did you work through any challenges internally, or how did you build support internally for a sustainability strategy?

Christine: I viewed the sustainability space more from a business perspective. I'm not an environmental scientist. I didn't grow up in public and corporate and governmental affairs dealing with stakeholders and NGOs. I'm more about triangulating data and thinking about what sustainability means from a variety of angles—environmental, social, consumer, and business.

For a business to take on an issue and commit to making a difference, I think it has to be integral to its business.

For Cocoa Life, that's exactly the connection we were able to find.

When I first got into this role, I went to some of the places where we source ingredients. I went to Ghana to see cocoa farms and meet the farmers. Before those visits, our marketing and business teams who manage the P&L had little exposure to what happens on the ground. We'd forecast our volume, all the ingredients would magically show up and meet our price and product specifications, and voilà—products get made and they go out the door. That's about the level of consciousness we had.

During my visits to those farms, I took tons of pictures and put together a presentation on the state of the cocoa supply chain for our folks who run our chocolate business and said, "You've got to see this. I'm going to pull back the curtain and show you." I then asked, "What are we going to go do about this? I want to commit to a journey to figure out a solution," and they fully supported it. That was the beginning of Cocoa Life, our commitment to ensuring a sustainable future for chocolate.

Derrick: Can you describe some key moments from Cocoa Life early on?

Christine: Mondelēz is one of the world's biggest buyers of cocoa, and we are facing significant environmental and social challenges. So I gathered a team and used white space innovation training, where you just dig in and look at a situation from a lot of different perspectives.

First, we looked at what was working. At the time, we were buying certified cocoa from Rainforest Alliance, we were buying from Fair Trade, and we had a Cadbury Cocoa Partnership in Ghana. We met several times with those groups and worked really hard with a cross-functional team that consisted of different internal disciplines, as well as external experts on issues like child labor, deforestation, and climate. This was nine years ago when we didn't even realize that the challenges were as big as they are.

Out of that analysis, we gleaned some insights from the Cadbury Cocoa Partnership that we might be able to scale. We created a 10-year P&L plan, and when we launched Cocoa Life in 2012, we committed $400 million over 10 years. It was just like a new product innovation, but instead of calculating how many packages of cookies run off the production line, it was, "How many tons of cocoa do we need? How much yield do we think we can get per tree? How many trees per origin need to be planted to rejuvenate the farms? Cost per tree? How long does it take for the trees to mature? How much farmer training is needed?"

I think this is part of why the business was willing to invest the money, because we did lots and lots of painstaking work and had check-ins along the way up to our CEO. I give so much credit to Irene Rosenfeld, who was our CEO at the time, for saying yes to the investment. For us, having our own teams on the ground where we work was a real departure in how we were going to behave, and it makes all the difference.

Ongoing strong support from our C-suite continues to reinforce the importance of our work. This year, Dirk Van de Put, our current Chairman and CEO, visited Cocoa Life farms and communities to see the program in action, and met with government leaders in Ghana and Côte d'Ivoire.

Derrick: Has Cocoa Life shifted or changed dramatically since it started?

Christine: Today, we're sourcing 45% of our chocolate brands through the program. We spent a lot of time up front defining what's required to be a sustainably sourced Cocoa Life bean: training farmers, working with farmers and, importantly, doing community action plans where we work with NGO partners because they're the experts in bringing together all the voices from the communities in Ghana, Côte d'Ivoire, Indonesia, etc. in a culturally relevant, local way. It's about a year-long process before all the boxes are checked off for the cocoa to qualify as Cocoa Life and be included in our volume. We have the process and transactions with farmers independently verified for accountability and transparency.

We're teaching people to fish versus giving them a fish. We help the communities learn how to draw on all their members and collectively develop a community action plan, like a strategic road map, of what they want for themselves and how to get there.

So now, seven years after launching, 45% of our cocoa meets all those requirements, and we're scaling up to be at 100% by the end of 2025. We're working with 143,000 farmers in almost 1,500 communities. We published our first-ever impact report this year instead of just a progress report. The learnings confirmed we are seeing progress on the ground across our KPIs. Importantly, we also understand what's working and what we need to accelerate, and that there's no way we're going to solve these challenges by ourselves. The data reinforced the important role governments need to play, the way industry needs to join forces, and where we need more donor support. Now we're embarking on bringing in more of those partners and having more of an advocacy voice on the issues.

Derrick: Wonderful. Congratulations on all the success.

Christine: Oh, thank you. It's a labor of love. One of the most satisfying experiences I had was in Côte d'Ivoire, probably my third visit. When we visit the origins, we try to see farming communities and farmers at different stages in the program. So we were there with some of our advisors at a meeting with one of the longer-term communities. It was so exciting and fulfilling because this community leadership team was pretty gender-balanced. It was about 50-50. And they just had such . . . the only word that comes to my mind is empowered. They embodied an empowered community, which is exactly what we want. Women were speaking, men were speaking . . . It's hard to describe, but it was just such a moving experience to see. Wow. You do all this theory and you do all this work, but to see it affecting people's lives, livelihoods, communities, and really driving change for the better is just so gratifying and so inspiring.

Derrick: Let's touch on the consumer side. I know the Cocoa Life mark is on some of the products. Are you getting any feedback from consumers about it?

Christine: We're still in the early days of the whole consumer journey. As we scaled Cocoa Life, we started with the on-the-ground work, building interventions, implementing them, and then scaling them to have enough cocoa to supply our brands. We have developed a global brand road map that guides us in terms of which brands go first as we flow the cocoa into our system.

Our brands are beginning to tell their consumers about Cocoa Life. Cadbury Dairy Milk has featured Cocoa Life for a couple years, and all Cadbury's product lines are now scaling up to be part of Cocoa Life. Milka joined last year.

> *"Do I spend money in advertising, or do I spend money investing in the cocoa farmers so that they can be sustainable, have better futures, and be in this with us as partners for the long haul?"*

I think consumers would be happy to know that all of the money, the $400 million we're spending on this sustainability program, comes out of the brand's P&L. That's one reason Cocoa Life is so distinctive. We don't have a foundation or a corporate fund. Instead, our brand leaders choose to invest in our cocoa supply chain and cocoa farmers so that they can be sustainable, have better futures, and be partners with us over the long term. That's why we're making this investment. As consumers learn more, I think it will build positive equity for our brands.

Derrick: If you were at another multinational company that's just starting to consider creating a social initiative from conception to where you are now, what advice would you share?

Christine: There are two pieces of advice I would give. When you have a program the scale and investment of Cocoa Life, having a way to evaluate its impact is critical. I believe our commitment to continuous learning—to trying things on the ground and having a way to assess the impact to know if something's working, what to accelerate, what to adjust—enables us to improve the effectiveness of the program.

The second is the importance of collaboration between

industry and governments because the challenges are too great to solve on one's own. We've been part of industry coalitions for several years now through the World Cocoa Foundation. The Cocoa & Forests Initiative is one example where we're working with about 35 companies and the Ghanaian and the Ivorian governments on a common approach and plan to tackle deforestation and environmental issues in those two countries. It's a shift for some companies who think we're all competitors, but sustainability is not the area to win market share. So I advise companies to embrace the idea that we all work and win together. It's really a lot more impactful. Because again, no one company is going to solve these challenges on their own.

Derrick: Anything else you think that we haven't talked about that you'd like to discuss?

Christine: Two more aspects to social impact. One is the role of business on social issues. I almost think sometimes it's easier for companies to think about, "Okay, well, health and wellness: That's one to tackle because it's directly connected to our products and our product attributes. Okay, check. Then environmental: well, I can see the impact that our supply chains and our manufacturing operations have on the environment. Check." But I think the social side is about understanding the interconnectedness . . . We're making products that come from ingredients, and that's somebody's livelihood. Again, it's about all of us along the value chain winning together. That doesn't just mean Mars and Nestlé and Hershey winning together with Mondelēz. It means the cocoa farmers having a livelihood and being partners with us in a vibrant supply chain. We're in this for the long haul, and we want them to be in it for the long haul with us.

The other social impact piece is how we help consumers. One

of the things we're working on is this whole idea of mindfulness. We are increasingly working on ways to help consumers snack mindfully—again, raising that consciousness to thinking about why you're eating something, and whether you're pausing for a moment in your day to really enjoy the pleasure of food so that you don't over-consume.

We sometimes get questions like, "Why would a company like yours tell us to be mindful about what we're eating and how we're eating? Isn't that kind of contradictory?" But we genuinely want to empower consumers to snack right. Oreo is over 100 years old, right? We want to have consumers be balanced, healthy, and feel like they can embrace our products and teach their children how to enjoy them for a very long time.

Overall, I think there are a lot of dimensions of social impact that companies can have. Businesses need to be working in these areas. Consumers expect us to work in those areas. Governments do; investors do with the rise of Environmental, Social and Governmental ESG initiatives. I think it's a terrific opportunity and one that will only grow for our company, not diminish.

Derrick: Has your company revised its original purpose? I think I heard that recently.

Christine: Yes. About a year ago, we launched this company purpose of "snacking made right." It's a declaration to the world of what we want to stand for: leading the future of snacking by helping people snack on the right snack in the right moment made in the right way. It has been definitely a catalyst for us to further accelerate our sustainability and well-being efforts.

CHAPTER 5

Trait 5: A Corporate Social Mind Has a Social Voice

Along with transparency, having an authentic voice on societal issues is vital to ensuring consumers, people, and stakeholders understand a company's views and values. Having a voice on an issue doesn't require the issue to be relatable to the company's product; the issue may simply affect the people within the company's community.

Businesses focused on social change today have a tremendous opportunity: Consumers and the general public are eager to engage, but their willingness to become involved with a company's efforts comes with specific expectations of intentionality, authenticity, and inclusiveness.

A company's role in social change should be that of an authentic voice speaking up for issues, but not one that thrusts itself into the role of omnipotent leader. Your voice should lead to a better understanding of an issue plaguing society; speaking with authenticity, accuracy, and transparency will result in consumers who are better informed about *you* as well as the *issue*.

FOCUS

Using one's voice requires a strategic and intentional approach— especially when the company needs to maintain sincerity and authenticity with the public. In this chapter, we will cover the following:

- When should we support the work of others in the community and lend our voice to an issue?
- What is possible for the company to perform on an issue and remain authentic to our values and position?
- How do we enter into public discourse about an issue?

From small family businesses to the largest corporations in their sector, companies are choosing to take a stand and have a voice on societal issues. Here are just a few:

SALESFORCE: AGAINST DISCRIMINATION BASED ON SEXUAL ORIENTATION

In 2015, then-Indiana Gov. Mike Pence was about to sign into law the Religious Freedom Restoration Act (RFRA), a measure that would allow businesses to discriminate against people based on their sexual preferences. Marc Benioff, CEO and chairman of Salesforce, knew his Indiana-based employees and clients would be adversely affected. He'd been among the legislation's many critics who were ignored by the majority of state legislators.

The day before the governor was scheduled to sign RFRA into law, Benioff decided to use all the weight of his global company, whatever the risk, to defend a cause he believed in.

First, he pledged to scale back Salesforce's significant investment in the state. When Pence signed the bill anyway, Benioff announced via Twitter he'd cancel all company programs that required customers or employees to travel to Indiana—a tweet shared 9,800 times and favorited 8,300 times. With still no movement by Pence, Benioff promised his Indiana employees a relocation package if they wanted to transfer to another state.

Salesforce became part of the national conversation surrounding this event and LGBTQ rights. Seeing his commitment, other major companies doing business in Indiana also acted: Angie's List put a proposed expansion on hold. Gen Con, a convention that draws over 60,000 people to the state capital, said it would consider changing locations. Yelp pledged to take pains not to establish offices in states with similar laws. A PayPal co-founder asked his fellow CEOs to rethink their business relationships with Indiana. The support from influential people and businesses mounted, as did the global media coverage.

It worked. On April 2, a mere seven days after he signed the original law, Pence signed a new measure passed by the legislature clarifying that RFRA would not permit discrimination based on gender identity or sexual orientation.

SIEMENS: A SOLUTION FOR REFUGEES AND INCREASED DEMANDS ON CITY INFRASTRUCTURE

In 2015, Germany became the European country that had welcomed the most refugees from Africa, Asia, and the Middle East, accepting four times their total number from a year earlier. At times, this meant up to 10,000 people every day arriving tired, hungry, homeless, and likely unable to communicate easily with local residents.

Siemens (whose products comprise systems and services for power generation, building technology, and integrated healthcare) wanted to do more than contribute to refugee camps or food pantries. It knew these refugees would need a way to support themselves. So Siemens created internship and training programs for those who applied for asylum there. Through work experience, intensive language instruction, and pre-vocational training in mechanics and electronics, Siemens placed participants in apprenticeship training positions. Employees voluntarily served as communication ambassadors and conducted fundraising campaigns; they also opened a company sports complex to refugee families and organized a shuttle bus to transport them.

But Siemens didn't stop there. It recognized that some German cities would struggle to serve this massive influx of new residents because their infrastructure had been built for smaller populations with different needs. Exacerbating those challenges was the fact that these cities had limited access to funds and financing; some even lacked basic legal frameworks needed to get involved in capital markets. Siemens partnered with PwC and Berwin Leighton Paisner to build "effective, efficient and sustainable urban infrastructure . . . from which economic success can grow."[1]

These partners' goals were to establish "Investor Ready Cities" by improving infrastructures in transport and mobility, energy, water and sanitation, and creating a safe and secure environment.

AD COUNCIL AND CORPORATE PARTNERS: HOW LOVE HAS NO LABELS CHANGED THE HEARTS AND MINDS OF THE PUBLIC AND EMPOWERED COMPANIES TO TAKE ACTION ON DIVERSITY AND INCLUSION

In 2015, division, bias, and discrimination were some of the most pressing issues facing the nation. Even more than in previous years, the numbers of hate crimes were soaring. The Supreme Court was slated to rule on marriage equality. Many groups felt increasingly marginalized and unsafe. Yet most Americans considered themselves to be unprejudiced because they didn't see themselves as part of the problem or recognize that they could be part of the solution by actively coming together and living inclusively.[2]

In an effort to promote acceptance and inclusion across race, age, gender, sexual orientation, ability, and religion, the Ad Council launched the Love Has No Labels campaign in 2015. The inaugural film for this campaign featured an X-ray screen that hid the identities of real people as they embraced, danced, and kissed. Viewers mentally filled in the blanks for what constituted friendship, romantic love, and family. When, at a later point in the film, the couples were revealed, so too were individual biases, as each relationship spanned different religions, races, disabilities, and more, demonstrating to viewers that "love has no labels." In only a few months, the campaign video achieved over 110 million views and started to shift attitudes and behaviors surrounding diversity and inclusion.

The campaign was further brought to life by an unprecedented collaboration of iconic brands, including The Coca-Cola Company, PepsiCo, P&G, Unilever, Allstate, State Farm, Bank of America, Wells Fargo, Budweiser, Google, and Johnson & Johnson. Over the years, these leading brands united in solidarity to support the campaign and use the Love Has No Labels platform as a way to actively engage with others both online and offline through social messaging, custom content creation, employee engagement, events, and more.

DICK'S SPORTING GOODS: A STAND ON GUN SAFETY

On Valentine's Day in 2018, a gunman killed 17 high school students in Parkland, Florida. Within two weeks, the CEO of Dick's Sporting Goods, Edward Stack, said Dick's stores (and its Field & Stream sites) would stop selling assault-style weapons and high-capacity magazines, and they wouldn't sell any gun to a person under 21. Stack said he'd been inspired by the activism of Parkland students following the shooting and wanted to help get a national conversation going about gun safety. It was a gutsy move for the largest sporting goods retailer in the country.

TRAIT 5 IN ACTION

These stories demonstrate the influence companies can have when they lend their voice and platform to a cause they feel passionate about. Each of them had business considerations to weigh alongside potential benefits to the cause. Each chose to get involved in a meaningful way—staking time, money, and reputation on what they believed in.

They recognized a need and asked themselves, "What do we stand for as a business?"

Choose Your Voice

As we've shown, corporate social impact work (CSR/ESG) is an intentional business strategy toward a social, political, and/or cultural goal. To lead our companies to act as responsible citizens of the world, we must make intentional decisions toward that end, and not aim solely for increased consumer loyalty.

Not every company has to be a Dick's Sporting Goods. The company watched its sales fall slightly after removing targeted weapons from its stores, but it stuck to its beliefs. Businesses and their leaders can assume one of three roles with their corporate voice to forward the cause:

Leading voice—Using your entire company platform to drive change

Contributing voice—Lending your knowledge and support to existing issues where it's critically needed

Supporting voice—Showing up with resources, the weight of your reputation, and other forms of support without speaking

You are a member of the communities in which you operate and where your employees, customers, vendors, and partners live and work. You ask something of these people, and you have a responsibility to stand up for those who cannot do it themselves.

Fortunately, standing up for others and creating new opportunities for an individual's voice to be heard is an authentic way to help your audiences understand, appreciate, and identify with the values underpinning your business.

Using your voice to leverage social change around an issue can be an enormous asset to a cause. When used in combination with other assets, the sky's the limit to what can be achieved.

Companies can progress in an authentic and strategic manner for social impact in six meaningful ways.

AUTHENTIC IMPACT IN SIX MEANINGFUL WAYS

1. LISTEN.

It's imperative to listen to and understand conversations that are already happening around the social issue you've chosen to champion. Becoming informed is vital to acting appropriately and authentically. As you listen, consider the roles your company can play to have impact: a participant at the table, an issue leader, an organizer.

2. MINGLE.

In concert with listening, go out among the people who are working to create change and among the beneficiaries of the work. Make an effort to understand how these already-engaged leaders, stakeholders, and causes create change, as well as what is actually needed to transform the population you're ultimately trying to serve. Consider how the company's voice can leverage the three aspects of issue engagement: public awareness, public adoption, and public action.

3. RESEARCH LANGUAGE AND STORIES.

Developing a good idea of the language, concerns, and passion points surrounding an issue can help you tell effective stories later, as well as decide ahead of time your stance/response to highly charged issues. This may be an area where your company's resources and professionalism can have enormous influence. Moreover, gaining an overall understanding of your issue's history, current status, and impending influences can help you avoid overpowering the conversation and, instead, dramatize the issue in an unforgettable way. Using your voice to leverage social change is an asset that should be used in combination with other assets for peak effectiveness.

4. KEEP A LOW(ER) PROFILE.

Be cognizant of your company's visibility. The issue isn't about your business; it's about who is being helped, challenged, and/or impacted. Even if your activities help your business or demonstrably boost a cause, be extremely cautious about taking credit. You'll be most successful when supporters, consumers, and your audiences feel directly connected to those they're helping—without you standing in the way. Create plans that incorporate the active use of the company's relationships, media, and communication channels, along with other methods of social change such as dollars, people, and time.

5. BE BRAVE.

Your role as a leader in the community is to stand for those not able to stand for themselves. This means you must be active in the good and boring times as well as the bad and negatively high-profile times. Companies must be bold in their cause work to influence today's younger demographic with its demands for authenticity and transparency. Consistent courage informed by facts is an authentic emotion that inspires respect, trust, and action in others.

continued

6. ASK FOR ACTION.

Today, businesses must do more than ask Americans or Europeans to notice their support of an issue and purchase their product because of it. Companies must ask the public to take some literal action—preferably with their peers—that allows them to demonstrate their own commitment to the issue while advancing it.

Creating a new opportunity for an individual's voice is a way to help them and others understand the values a company stands for. By giving people a concrete action to perform to help the cause, you'll be doing more than you realize to advance your company. Be sure to prepare a plan of measuring these actions, from calls to action to response to impact.

TRAIT 5:
Design and Innovation Questions

To create a plan that incorporates the active use of company relationships and media and communication channels along with other components of social change, such as dollars, people, and time, consider asking these questions first to leverage three aspects of issue engagement:

- Public awareness—How will we help others in the public understand this issue?
- Public adoption—How will we change perceptions, attitudes, and beliefs within and outside the company on this issue?
- Public action—What are we asking the public to do to show support for the issue?

If you engage people in your cause work in this way, you will build the relationships, loyalty, interest, and affinity you desire while influencing an issue that's relevant and important to the public and consumers alike.

Jennifer Foyle, Aerie

"We set out to promote female empowerment and inclusive body images—and along the way, the Aerie brand has ushered in a new era of authenticity that has unleashed the power of real, unretouched women."

JEN FOYLE describes how Aerie took a risk in using its platform to reveal that beauty standards for girls and women are artificially created. In this interview, she shares why she believes so strongly in building a team from within to support the brand and mission, and how she did it at Aerie.

Derrick: Will you describe your role at Aerie and how you engage with social issues?

Jen: I've had a pretty successful career in retail for 26 years. I took this job with Aerie in 2010, and it has been a labor of love. The magic moment came in 2014. Aerie was developing this amazing product, and we had a team in place with passion to grow the brand. We're here, we're doing this. But the thought came: What else can we do for our customers? That's when the creative team presented me with an unbelievable concept.

I was reviewing a floor set and in-store marketing when my team said, "We don't know if you realize it, but these models have not been airbrushed." It was the "wow" moment. If a model is a model for a profession, why would anyone airbrush her? So we created a huge campaign around this idea of real, unretouched beauty. And now, this little idea has turned into so much more—it's a movement.

The evolution of #AerieREAL is what makes the brand's marketing and the connection with our customers so magical. Last year, for instance, we asked our customers to submit video and stories for the fall 2018 campaign. It was so emotional and special. In the end, we received more than 1,800 submissions representing an incredible populace of women of all ages and with unique stories—breast cancer survivors, young moms, girls suffering from diabetes, and those with special needs. It was remarkable. We set out to promote female empowerment and inclusive body images—and along the way, the Aerie brand has ushered in a new era of authenticity that has unleashed the power of real, unretouched women.

I am so proud that Aerie has been a pioneer in the body positivity and inclusivity moment. We are paralleling a social transformation, particularly within the fashion industry. I think we owe it to all women and to our customers to do more. We want women to feel good about their real selves. There's certainly more work to do, and at Aerie, we understand the importance of challenging the stereotypical standards of beauty—which gives our customers a voice.

Derrick: So before this, had Aerie taken on any other social issues?

Jen: No. We had just begun building the brand, and the launch of #AerieREAL in 2014 was transformational for so many reasons. My daughter was seven at the time, and one day as we were standing in front of the mirror, she said, "Mom, am I beautiful?" My daughter's need to even ask me that question was sobering. The light bulb went off. My personal life and my work were converging in this deeply personal way, and I knew I wasn't alone. I knew the Aerie brand was onto something really special.

Derrick: Was there any pushback internally at all about moving in this direction? And you're a nationwide consumer brand, right? You've got individuals in all parts of the country, in the world. How was the consumer response?

Jen: The Aerie brand has been given so much runway for success. Internally, when we presented the idea to forgo retouching, the leadership team simply said, "It's about time."

The positive outpouring of stories and empowerment we hear from our customers daily is a constant reminder that the Aerie brand truly is helping to change the way young girls and women see themselves.

Derrick: Along the way, have you ever learned something that made you modify the campaign or the initiative overall?

Jen: For Aerie, it's all about challenging the status quo and never settling. We are always forging ahead, but what we've learned is to protect the DNA of our brand. We're real with our customers but most importantly ourselves. We never waiver. No retouching. Only body confidence and empowerment because we want everyone to feel confident inside and out.

Derrick: How did the nonprofit side respond to a brand taking this on like you have?

Jen: Our first #AerieREAL role model was Iskra Lawrence.

She's been through so much herself as a model. The trials and tribulations she's gone through—from being told she was too thin to being plus size, classified as overweight (which is ridiculous), trying to fit into a size that wasn't realistic, to having an eating disorder. Together, we've worked to challenge conventional beauty standards, build confidence, and celebrate the unique qualities that make us all beautiful.

Inspired by Iskra's experience and passion, Aerie has partnered with the National Eating Disorders Association (NEDA) since 2015 to reduce the stigma associated with eating disorders and reinforce a positive body image. We also have a long-standing partnership with Bright Pink, a preventive and awareness program that promotes the early detection of breast and ovarian cancer in young women. It's incredibly gratifying to know that through these two organizations, we've empowered millions of women within our #AerieREAL community to be proactive about their health and recognize the importance of self-wellness and self-love.

Derrick: If you had to summarize one or two things you think have made #AerieREAL so successful, what would they be?

Jen: We've built a team from within—a team with so much passion that they live and breathe #AerieREAL. They believe in the Aerie mission, create incredible product to make our customers feel good—inside and out—and they know we are just getting started. Everyone who touches the Aerie brand from our corporate associates, store teams, to ultimately our customers—everyone is a piece of what this brand has become and is helping to shape Aerie's future.

It's important to keep looking ahead and not looking back.

"At Aerie, we constantly ask what more could we be doing and whether what we're doing is real, because the customer will know immediately if it isn't authentic."

Derrick: A lot of people are trying to ease into social issues, especially given this climate today. You took on one that's potentially controversial. What advice would you give someone who wants to bring their brand into a potentially controversial conversation?

Jen: Customers today can spot a phony a mile away. You have to be committed from the inside out. At Aerie, we constantly ask what more could we be doing and whether what we're doing is real, because the customer will know immediately if it isn't authentic.

There has to be a level of passion around a great idea—you need the passion of more than one person, and getting a whole team rallied around a social cause takes endless work, day in and day out. It's a job inside a job. You better be sure you're committed to doing that.

Derrick: Has your work on #AerieREAL changed the way you view other brands that are getting involved in social issues?

Jen: I'm flattered that others have followed in Aerie's footsteps, which sounds vain and I don't mean it to be. Other brands that are continuing the conversation around inclusivity only further our mission. Like-minded brands and leaders can create impactful change and create a world where all people feel represented and included.

Derrick: What does the future for #AerieREAL look like? What would you love to accomplish next?

Jen: This is more than just a job. At some point in my career, I realized I want to succeed, I want to do well, but I can't be just "I" alone. I want to be with a team that's always looking for the next window or space to embrace new ideas and new social happenings or new ways we can help solve new issues.

But what's next? I mean, we have so much more to do! Sustainability is incredibly important to the Aerie team. There's lots of work to do around fabrics, manufacturing, packaging . . . the list goes on . . . and I'd like to start tackling it because it's up to all of us to do our part to build a better world for future generations.

CHAPTER 6

Trait 6: A Corporate Social Mind Leads Social Collectives

Companies lead and engage by driving the agenda of social issue collectives. These collectives include representation from all the sectors that could make issue-related change happen.

Mark Parker, CEO of Nike, commented in a *Fast Company* article on the evolving nature of today's business: "The biggest sources of opportunity are collaboration and partnership. And today, with digital communication, there is more of that everywhere. We need to expose ourselves to that as a matter of doing business."[1]

It looks like he was right: Cooperation, competition, partnership, collaboration, alliance, stakeholder management, sharing, and collective impact are all concepts that stand for a culture of working together, of bringing parties with various backgrounds to the table where one plus one equals more than two.

Collaboration is often the key to facing up to societal challenges. You could argue that business has learned quite a bit over the years from the long tradition of collaborative cultures in civil society and government. Japanese poet Ryunosuke Satoro is known for his words where he summarized all this beautifully: "Individually, we are one drop. Together, we are an ocean."

Let us explore these seas.

FOCUS

When companies today get involved in issues like malaria, HIV, plastic in the oceans, climate change, better education locally, or community culture programs, often civil society organizations, academia, and government become important forces to work with in creating good. A culture of collaboration therefore must be another characteristic of a corporate social mind.

In this chapter, we will explore answers to the following questions:

- What are examples of the collaboration of companies, governmental agencies, causes, and the public in tackling a societal issue?
- What forms of cooperation are there?
- What are the conditions for a successful collaboration?
- Why are collaborations often more about trust than about tools, resources, or evidence?

TRAIT 6 IN ACTION

The following three companies took their own approaches to collaborations based on their products and operations.

Siemens Stiftung

Siemens Stiftung is an independent charitable foundation that acts as an important lever of societal change for Siemens, an engineering and technology company. One focus of the foundation is innovative approaches to science, technology, engineering, and math (STEM) education in primary and secondary schools. In collaboration with teachers, schools, researchers, municipalities, and regions, the foundation developed the evidenced-based curriculum *Experimento* for experienced-based learning that's now being used in classrooms in Bolivia, Chile, Colombia, Germany, Peru, Kenya, Mexico, and South Africa.

Benefits from this collaboration in Medellín, Colombia, extend far beyond an individual school. While many people still associate the city with drug trafficking, kidnappings, and guerrilla warfare, Siemens Stiftung and its local affiliate, the Siemens Fundación, are part of a larger alliance of city government, schools, civil society, and companies called Territorio STEM+H whose purpose is to improve the state of human and social development through STEM education.

The Siemens Fundación integrates its experiences in STEM education and its curriculum in this wider effort to improve the city's education system. Without such partnerships, the curriculum would be taught only in a couple of schools and would not be a part of a wider toolbox to improve a whole education landscape.

Ellen MacArthur Foundation

The New Plastics Economy of the Ellen MacArthur Foundation is the best-known collaboration for resolving the issue of plastics in the environment.[2] This initiative underlines the value in collaborations of a (neutral) convener or facilitator.

To create it, the foundation invited stakeholders from the business community—Amcor, Danone, H&M, L'Oréal, Mars, Novamont, PepsiCo, The Coca-Cola Company, Unilever, Veolia—to join political, academic, and civil society actors to collaborate on the implementation of a circular economy for plastic packaging. The New Plastics Economy has already published a variety of reports and, in collaboration with UN Environment, has initiated the New Plastics Economy Global Commitment, a common vision and set of targets to address plastics pollution. This global collaboration has even started to initiate "Plastic Pacts" to support implementation at national and regional levels.

The New Plastics Economy is a complex and multilevel collaboration closely connected to the core of participating businesses. Still, all players know that an issue like the eradication of plastic waste can be solved only if all stakeholders collaborate to identify innovations, improve regulations, etc.

BASF

Ludwigshafen is a city of 170,000 people in Rhein-Main, one of Germany's major economic and wine regions on the Rhine. But there is another city within this city. The chemical company BASF is based there and has developed the largest chemical production and research site in the world run by one company. Around 39,000 people work for BASF in more than 2,000 buildings, including a theatre and a concert hall. BASF has been a long-time provider and sponsor of cultural events in its community, viewing this support as an expression of corporate (cultural) social responsibility. The company's CSR team often brings together cultural players from all over the region to address issues together. In a current project, called Tor 4—named for the company's largest gate to the city—BASF has embarked on a new collaboration to connect its community involvement in the arts to societal issues that are important to local citizens. The first stage involved assembling representatives from the arts, academia, and politics to define themes around which the company will initiate dialogue, asking such thought-provoking questions as, "Why is everything getting better?" or "How does freedom really work?"

Tor 4 is based on a partnership and community approach on various levels. There is a steering committee that brings together politicians, business managers, and arts experts to ensure the relevance of the program for the community and its artistic aspirations. A small team within BASF coordinates the initiative and acts like a backbone organization for it. Most importantly, there are more than 16 cultural institutions that have designed and implemented artistic interventions all over the region.

We may not naturally connect the corporate social mind with an intense collaboration with the arts community, but the BASF Corporate Social Responsibility Team has found a way to expand its existing efforts to serve the broader community.

These three companies are not alone. More and more businesses today are working collaboratively on issues like water, organic cotton, and vaccination. The new global reality is to find joint solutions to pressing problems—some close to the business' core, some a lot closer to the overall concerns of society.

These examples from around the world show how and why collaboration and partnership must be part of the corporate social mind. To collaborate is not easy because it requires a dialogue and trust. Our work as facilitators in such alliances has clearly revealed their added value—and that in many instances, they are the only way to truly move an issue.

- **Collaboration:** Working with entities to pursue a one-time joint effort
- **Partnership:** Ongoing working relationship with shared risks and rewards
- **Network:** Professional and personal contacts that are often the basis for collaborations or partnerships
- **Collective:** Intentional working entity, often across sectors for a strategic and intentional social outcome

COLLABORATION OUTCOMES

In this section, we will identify four outcomes that often come from social-good collaborations. They are not mutually exclusive, and it's possible to target one or more of them in your planning.

1. **Mobilize access to resources that a single person or organization could not mobilize.** This can be the pooling of money, the sharing of experiences, knowledge or social capital, or the credibility and diverse representation that a wider stakeholder base creates for a cause.

2. **Initiate innovations.** Innovations often happen when experiences and new ideas are combined.[3] Collaboration often is a driver for innovation because it brings together

diverse points of view, knowledge, etc., sparking new ideas for new solutions.

3. **Increase the interaction between partners.** Collaboration offers many different means of working together, from face-to-face meetings and backbone organizations to facilitation and digital network management tools.[4]

4. **Create structures and processes that enable and streamline working together.** Collaboration promotes the exchange of information and thus becomes a driver of transparency.

Besides the potential issue solutions, these outcomes show the tremendous potential of organizations combining their voices, technology, innovation power, marketing skill, and people to pursue societal good. What management principles lie behind these ways of working together? Various evaluations and overall research on collaboration have repeatedly shown that the following principles are relevant:

1. There is a need to invest in human and organizational resources to build a collaborative network. It is crucial to continuously pursue activities within a collaborative setup and even to dedicate people and resources to it.

   • The members of the Medellín education initiative have pooled resources to create a dedicated organizational setup that drives the collaboration. Siemens Stiftung has dedicated staff that represent the foundation in the initiative.

- The New Plastics Economy initiative relies on the effort of all its members. Besides the core team put together by the Ellen MacArthur Foundation, many other network partners have committed staff or staff time for this endeavor.

2. Good process and quality management are critical for a collaboration's success. You need facilitation, transparent indicators for monitoring, and evaluation or project management.

- BASF's Tor 4 uses external facilitators for partner meetings and has decided on clear indicators for monitoring development.

3. The prerequisite is that the cause of a collaboration, its targets, and the overall setup, including available resources, are defined and agreed on by the partners.

- The Cotton 2040 "convening initiative" brings together 140 stakeholders from the textile industry. The initiative is funded by a consortium, especially from the business community, while the charitable Forum for the Future hosts, facilitates, and manages it. The initiative has developed clearly defined work streams to ensure the sourcing of enough sustainable cotton.

4. A good, efficient governance for such collaborations is one of the major challenges—especially since in these settings, worlds often come together that do not meet naturally. Clear, transparent direction and guidance in a setup based on participation and dialogue is key.

- The Tamarack Institute has initiated many collaborations between local government, business, and civil society.[5] It runs Vibrant Communities Canada: Cities Reducing Poverty, which has a clear network of overall governance and strives for that same transparency on every local level.

Trust is a vital resource you need to mobilize in collaborations. Working together also means letting go. It means issues are decided in a dialogue. It means you have to trust in relationships with your partners. Trust is fundamental to every collaborative effort.

> Collaboration well done enhances the potential efforts to make a change in the following ways:
>
> - **Outcome:** The effects an action has directly on the target audience of the program or product
> - **Impact:** The long-term or systemic effects of an action on society overall

COLLECTIVE IMPACT

These observations are parallel to the most common collaboration concept used in business right now: collective impact. John Kania and Mark Kramer, with social change consulting group FSG, identified the following criteria for collective impact initiatives:[6]

- A common agenda and goals of the actors.
- A shared and standardized metric for assessing progress and impact.
- Mutual support in each actor's activities, i.e.,

differentiated areas of expertise and activity according to individual strengths with close coordination.

- Consistent and open communication across the many players to build trust, assure mutual objectives, and appreciate common motivation.

- Shared and centralized infrastructure with highly motivated members providing coordination and support.

Effective social collaboratives have similar characteristics. Participants may have cultural variances, or the context for each may be different, but they all rely on a comparable playbook.

These collaborations often start out with an initiation phase in which targets, resources, and other frameworks are sorted out, normally ending in a contract or a Memo of Understanding and a set of common goals that are also communicated to the public. The collaboration is then free to pursue its targets and, with the help of monitoring and reporting tools, ensure participants and the overall effort stay on track. Time frames can differ; a collaboration to improve a school system is often a long-term project, while collaborations around a certain regulatory issue or something time sensitive can be brief. Sometimes, the result of a collaboration is an institutionalization of the effort to serve an ongoing need for dialogue and to monitor progress.

Most societal challenges demand a collaborative solution, as do most problems. The management of successful collaborations is defined by openness, transparency, tolerance, facilitation, authenticity, and reliability. The corporate social mind focuses on context and diversity.

OUR OWN COLLABORATION: RÖCHLING FOUNDATION

Concurrent with working on this book, we started a collaboration with the Röchling Foundation, the philanthropic arm of the family-owned business, Röchling SE & Co. KG. This global plastics engineering company based in southern Germany develops custom plastic products for industrial, automotive, and medical use.

When they came to Wider Sense, the foundation had decided to focus on how innovations in plastic emissions could help prevent negative environmental impacts.

Frankly, all of Wider Sense—our team and the foundation's manager and board chair—initially wondered if the issue was already being addressed by too many organizations for Röchling to have any impact. Did the world really need more awareness of plastics pollution? Would we be able to bring stakeholders to *our* particular table when many of them likely were already involved with this issue elsewhere?

The whole idea began to sound like the same old playbook we'd worked from many times before. In addition, since our first level of research identified many, many forums, expert committees, etc., related to the issue, we believed that the foundation surely wasn't needed as yet another solutions investigator.

We were wrong.

Before making a decision, we decided to conduct intensive research to thoroughly understand the plastics challenge as well as the needs of stakeholders. The result was the report *Polyproblem*, which breaks down the various levels of change in this arena.[7] The big surprise? Every single interviewee in the

continued

research process encouraged the foundation and the company to tackle bringing together three disparate sectors of stakeholders to explore solutions to plastics pollution: business, government, and civil society.

We now had a firm understanding of the nuances within the issue. We knew where change was and was not occurring. We had enthusiastic stakeholders urging us to pursue a joint solution. Therefore, to validate all this data one last time, we asked the foundation to invite its stakeholders to take part in dialogues around solutions for the prevention of plastic emissions.

The result: The foundation has begun a process to define a specific role for itself as a convener of collaborations to address plastics pollution.

TRAIT 6:
Design and Innovation Questions

The following questions can guide you and your business in assessing the need for a collaboration or partnership to address a community issue:

- Who are the stakeholders involved in the cause?
- Why are they involved?
- What are common interests of the stakeholders? Are they strong enough to define and support joint targets?
- How do we want to work together?
- Who are the leaders that can motivate a collaborative to thrive?
- Who are the leaders within our organization who will be champions of the collaboration?
- Who within our organization has a lot of experience with collaborations or the organizations we want to work with?
- What resources can our organization bring to the table?
- What is the time horizon of the collaboration?
- What is the right structure for the collaboration (contracts, meeting formats, etc.)?

Get ready to be part of an ocean in your local community, your region, your country, or your planet.

David Raper, IBM

"If you want to survive, if you want to thrive, you've got
to be doing this work in the 21st century."

DAVID RAPER, IBM's Director, Corporate Social Responsibility
North America & Social Impact Fund, explains how collaboration
is one principle for their social impact work.

Michael: Please describe your role at IBM and how you engage
with, lead, or design social impact work for the company.

David: I have two main roles at IBM. The first is leading our
CSR team across North America. We work with communities to
achieve social impact with technology, particularly in the areas
of education and skills, and also in support of IBM employees'
own volunteering and contributions back to their communities. That responsibility ladders up on the business side to goals
around improving IBM's reputation. That's one part.

Then the second part of my role is establishing a social impact
investing capability. We will be expanding from our Impact
Grants program, in which we provide grants very often to

not-for-profit organizations, to also include impact investing for start-up companies, social enterprises, and similar organizations.

Michael: What personal values drive you to do that kind of work, and how do these values intersect with your work at IBM?

David: I always had a very strong passion for creating an environment with opportunities for people and communities to really be their best. I'm also a very curious person. I like to understand different cultures, people, business models, and so that all comes together in the work at IBM or in social impact in many ways.

I feel privileged that because we're an outwardly facing function, we get to meet so many interesting people doing wonderful things in their communities and work with a lot of nonprofit organizations and support them in their mission. The emphasis of that work for us is on education, skills, and workforce and how we can build an inclusive workforce and digital economy. It aligns very much with my passion for opening up opportunities for inclusion.

Michael: What is the focus of IBM's social impact and sustainability work?

David: As a company we develop and, with our clients, deploy new and powerful technologies. It's really important to exercise responsible stewardship as we bring these technologies into the world, to usher them in safely, and to build an economy that's inclusive in their deployment and benefits.

CSR really does touch every part of the IBM company. For example, research at IBM is building AI models that can detect bias, explain it, and start to open up what's happening inside that AI black box. HR is about building a diverse workforce to ensure there's diversity in the development and design of these technologies. So social impact and the impact of our company on the world is something that IBM is conscious of across its business.

Michael: How would you see IBM's work on social impact CSR connected to the innovation capabilities of the company?

David: It's connected in a lot of reinforcing ways. First, our work in the community is a way of learning about the community. I hope that as we introduce impact investing, for instance, it will be another source of learning—for IBM, for CSR, and for our employees in general.

Second, as IBM is developing technologies, we want to make sure they're deployed responsibly. CSR is a way of demonstrating that this piece of technology or innovation actually has a role to play in creating a better world. So our social impact CSR is an integral part of practical projects and in demonstrating why they're needed.

Michael: Can you share the story of IBM's P-TECH schools?

David: We're very proud of P-TECH. A P-TECH school is a partnership between a school, a community college, and an industry entity that brings together the last four years of high school with two years of postsecondary school. Students graduate with both a high school diploma and an associate's degree in a field that is aligned to fast-growing STEM careers in their community.

And what's different about P-TECH is that it's very collaborative. So business and educators are sitting down every day to discuss the skill needs of industries, talk about how they map those throughout the entire six-year curriculum, and then identify gaps and collaboratively bridge them with innovative learning experiences.

It's a highly integrated program that creates pathways for students either into a job or on to further study. When they finish, graduates have (a) a lot of job-relevant skills, (b) an associate's degree, and (c) new networks that help link them to employment and opportunity. Especially for students coming from more disadvantaged areas and backgrounds, or families or communities that might not have those connections themselves, this program can be very powerful in terms of opening up young people's futures.

What we're trying to do is to create a systems change, more than just a school or curriculum, and reform what high school means in the 21st century. By the end of 2020, we'll have over 220 schools across 23 countries.

Michael: How important is it for you to look at impact?

David: It's very important. We look at metrics such as high school and college completion rates, grades, and attendance. In the first US schools that opened, college completion rates are four to five times higher than you would expect from similar cohorts.

I can also tell you that in a P-TECH school, you can see and hear the difference in the capabilities of the students in terms of their self-confidence, their ability to communicate, and their ability to articulate their goals in the pathway they're on. As a human being, you can feel the things we're measuring.

Michael: How do you measure? Do you do external evaluations or do it internally with defined indicators?

David: At the moment, we measure internally using those indicators. It's also very much going to be working with education departments globally to build a data set for all P-TECH schools.

Michael: How would you describe the effect of such an initiative as P-TECH on the company and its employees?

David: What we hear is that it has big effects in a number of ways. Internally, we know that employees really enjoy being P-TECH mentors and building relationships with students, sharing what they know, and providing advice about what it's like to work in a company like IBM and what the pathway might be to get the job.

Also, as we hire people from often-different backgrounds who might not as easily find a way into a company like IBM, it is really helping to improve our diversity.

> *"You're going to be more effective at social initiatives the more they play to the things that your company is good at."*

Michael: If you were to advise somebody who wants to start social impact work from the beginning, what are the two things you would tell them?

David: If I could say only two things, they would be this: Number one, prioritize the issues. There are many, many issues in the communities in which we operate and various ways to address them. Prioritizing helps make sure you're not spread too thin.

Second, choose areas that have business relevance to your company, and by that, I mean two things: One is that it's important to the company, because that will help make it sustainable so the company will help you grow the function over time. Number two: Think about relevance in terms of the capabilities of your company. IBM has certain capabilities around technology, for example, and we really leverage those heavily in our CSR. You're going to be more effective at social initiatives the more they play to the things that your company is good at.

Michael: What management principles or tools have helped you in your work? Are there one or two principles that were really important to the work?

David: I use concepts around adaptive leadership, change management, and stakeholder relations. When you're doing significant work, often you and the company and the community all need to evolve in order to be successful. For example, with something like P-TECH, it includes looking internally and asking, does every job need a four-year degree, or can we define roles in which a two-year qualification is more appropriate? That requires some changes in everyone's thinking.

Michael: What would you say is the most important argument for a company to work in the social space?

David: If you want your company to survive, if you want it to thrive, you've got to do it. The expectations on companies from the community are rising exponentially. When I say "the community," I mean the general public, consumers, investors, employees, as well as regulators. There is great transparency into what companies are doing and how they're behaving.

CHAPTER 7

Trait 7: A Corporate Social Mind Measures Social Impact

C ompanies with a corporate social mind measure the impact of their decisions on all aspects of society as well as on their business. An intentional focus on transparency is present where a culture of reporting finances, societal impact, product developments, and impact on people and planet is normalized.

Two often-heard quotes juxtaposed may best illustrate the challenge of measuring the social impact of a company. Physicist Albert Einstein supposedly said, "Not everything that counts can be counted, and not everything that can be counted counts." Many of us intuitively agree. The effects of an anti-bullying program in a school are so much more than the number of students physically protected. Anti-bullying programs, for instance, may also have an effect on the overall school climate or even health choices of students. A corporate volunteering program in a homeless shelter is not only about the number of meals colleagues have handed out. The program may encourage employees to volunteer long term with the shelter and also may have a team-building effect on the colleagues that took part in the engagement.

A CEO who stands up for innovative, sustainable ways to package a product may create ripples locally, nationally, and even globally for people and the planet. The interview with Rüdiger Fox from Sympatex (following chapter 1) shows how a bold decision on the sustainability principles of a product can create such a disruption for an industry—even though it may take time to scale.

In the business world, most people prefer to adhere to another quote, this one by management thinker Peter Drucker: "What gets measured gets managed."[1] You may also know the adaptation of this quote, "What gets measured gets done." This cause-effect relationship of measurement seems obvious. But looking deeper, especially when it comes to work for the community or the environment, the effects are a lot more complex, diverse, and sometimes even unintended.

Much of management is about things such as reporting, counting, and norms. Consider the production of a car: On the one hand, it's defined by the art of engineering; on the other hand, it reflects the drive of management to be as efficient as possible in its production. But the ultimate unit of measurement on both sides is generally the manufacturing cost of producing the car. Drucker, in contradiction to everything professionals in the business have projected onto his work, observed that this is never the case.

His example is the analysis of the accidents caused by a car, concluding, "Finding the appropriate measurement is not a mathematical exercise. It is a risk-taking judgment."[2] A "risk-taking judgment" means taking a big leap from one number, cost, or efficiency. It is the consideration of a measurement that is much more in line with observing, understanding, and measuring the impact of the social engagement of a company.

FOCUS

The concept of measurement is highly contested when it comes to corporate management. For some it is an *Unwort* (German for "an ugly word"), and for others it's a magic formula. The distance between these poles seems to rapidly increase many times when dealing with the social engagement of companies. How can you measure actual impact of social engagement?

In this chapter, we explore answers to the following questions:

- Why is measuring the impact of a company's social engagement such a challenge?
- What are basic concepts to use for tackling this challenge?
- How will this field change with the growing availability of data on societal issues?
- Why should we still be cautious and accept limits to measurement in this field?

TRAIT 7 IN ACTION

Measurement is normally driven by the urge to do better. Today, in many areas of the business world, it is part of the legal framework within which companies operate. In Europe, Directive 2014/95/EU requires large companies to publish regular reports on the social and environmental impact of their activities, and companies and accountants in Europe have explored a variety of ways to comply with this directive over the years. Indexes such as the Dow Jones Sustainability Index ask companies around the world to report on their social engagement, though it cannot require them to do so. A growing number of national legislative bodies globally ask for similar social engagement documentation:

- Netherlands and United States: If you do not document a certain amount of pro bono staff hours, your company is ineligible for public contracts.

- South Africa: Since 2008, regulations implementing Companies Act No. 71 specify expectations and amounts of community reinvestment for companies. The King Report on Corporate Governance for South Africa 2016 ("The King IV Report") further expands on that by including concrete expectations for companies to give back to the communities they do business in.

- India: The Indian government enacted Section 135 of the Companies Act in 2013, which legally requires companies doing business in India to spend 2% of average net profits on community engagement.

These are only a handful of the external and legal frameworks supporting social engagement around the globe today.

Stringent internal measures already exist, because it's clear that societal engagement effects a company's innovation capacity, its risk/reputation management, the quality of management, and likely its overall income. But social issue engagement and related partnerships make sense *only* if the impact is real. What does this mean for the management of social engagement measurement?

MANAGING SOCIAL ENGAGEMENT MEASUREMENT

We start our hands-on expedition into the measurement of a company's social engagement in Granada, Spain. Granada has a rich and turbulent history. A lively crossroad of cultures in the early Middle Ages, today the city is a sparkling university town, business hub, and popular destination for research conferences.

In September 2013, the Mondelēz International Foundation piggybacked an event onto the International Congress of Nutrition in Granada that explored ways to measure the impact of its global social engagement. The foundation's vision saw the evolution of the metrics of individual NGO partners into a shared set of global metrics that could be tracked and measured by all partners.

Mondelēz, one of the largest foods-producing companies in the world, focuses its social engagement on the well-being of children in local communities. Mondelēz partners with local not-for-profit organizations that deliver nutrition education while promoting active play and/or providing access to fresh foods for children. (At the time, Mondelēz's well-being program was in its beginning stages. Today, it encompasses partnerships in more than 18 countries.)

What do the NGO partners of the Mondelēz International Foundation actually do? Two examples can illustrate just that:

- Klasse2000 is a healthy lifestyle education non-profit reaching more than 16,000 primary-school classrooms in Germany every year. Evidence-based educational interventions teach students about self-esteem, healthy eating, and the importance of exercise and movement.

- The China Youth Development Foundation supports school students mainly in rural China with equipment and training for school staff. The goal is to provide better-quality food, but also to ensure students get ample time to move and play during their school day.

Back to 2013. As one of the largest producers of snacks, Mondelēz has always made clear its commitment to children growing up learning about and living a healthy lifestyle—facing head-on the paradox often perceived between its products (e.g., cookies, chocolate) and its social engagement.

The representatives of the NGOs came prepared to the event in Granada. They had been mentored by experts to develop a theory of change for their work with children and youth. ("Theory of change" is field jargon for a strategy development tool that defines long-term goals and conditions necessary to reach each goal.)[3] Attending NGO representatives explained their reporting metrics and shared how the foundation's input had affected their work and impacted children.

The event ended with participants identifying an initial set of measurements to be used consistently by the foundation and all NGO partners. In its *Impact for Growth 2017* progress report, Mondelēz listed the following indicators for healthy lifestyle education that was derived from the Granada workshop:

1. Nutrition Knowledge: Percentage of program participants who improve their nutrition knowledge.

2. Physical Activity: Percentage of participants who are physically active for 30 minutes or more daily.

3. Healthier Eating: Percentage of participants who report increased consumption of fruits, vegetables, and other fresh foods.[4]

These indicators are now standard measures in the field. The World Health Organization uses them to assess the effectiveness of healthy lifestyle education interventions.

The Mondelēz International Foundation's approach to developing a joint understanding of their collaborative initiative combined a variety of features important for assessing societal engagement.

SOCIAL ENGAGEMENT MEASUREMENT BY MONDELĒZ INTERNATIONAL FOUNDATION

- The foundation selected one method to work with consistently and secured the backing (for credibility and expertise) of a health sector-specific evaluation researcher.
- The foundation provided capacity-building support for its partners to implement data collection in their own work.
- The NGOs and other stakeholders were asked to participate in theory-of-change and measurement framework development. Such participation is crucial for ultimate success.
- The foundation continues to use these methods and indicators to plan its work. Measurement of societal engagement makes sense only if you integrate it into your strategic and implementation planning.
- The tool and indicators allow the foundation to monitor and report on its initiative in a transparent and comprehensible way to shareholders, management, the media, and the wider public.

THE IOOI METHOD

For those who work in the space of social impact and corporate social responsibility, four words come up repeatedly: input, output, outcome, and impact (IOOI). This so-called IOOI approach to social impact measurement is currently the most widely used in the corporate world.

- **Input** describes the resources a company has invested. These resources can be financial capital (donations, investments), social capital (networks, contacts), intellectual capital (skill and time of your employees), and/or emotional capital (trust).

- The accomplishments that result from the use of these resources are countable measures or **output**. In the case of the Mondelēz International Foundation, these could be the number of trainings delivered or the number of children reached. In others, they could be the number of mosquito nets distributed or the hours employees volunteered for an NGO.

- The effects intervention has directly on the target audience of the program and/or the company are called **outcomes**. An outcome could be a better housing situation for homeless people after a donation-funded shelter expansion. Another could be improved volunteer training skills through holding mock job interviews with unemployed youth. An outcome could be the leveraging effect of introducing corporate volunteers to an engagement opportunity for refugees or an environmental cause.

- The long-term effects of an intervention on society overall is the **impact**. This could be better quality of life and health of children in an educational program, finding a job after a training program run by corporate volunteers, or the long-term results of improved air, better access to energy, and clean and closer drinking water.[5-7]

In the last couple of years, companies have developed many ways to describe and measure the effects of their societal engagement. As we've mentioned, you can now find these results in many companies' corporate social responsibility or sustainability reports.

When the French multinational company Schneider Electric SE reports on its community initiatives in the field of energy and fuel poverty, its outcome indicators are clearly defined by the number of "underprivileged people trained in energy management" and "mission within Schneider Electric Teachers NGO."[8] Both indicators are consistent with the company's strategy to create better access to energy through its core business activities as well as through corporate volunteering, corporate foundation grants, and the company's social investment fund. This may not seem spectacular on its face, but in 2019, Schneider Electric was named one of *Fortune* magazine's most admired companies in the world and one of the most ethical companies by Ethisphere Institute.

SOCIAL MEASUREMENT AS PART OF THE BUSINESS CASE

Dutch start-up Justice42 takes the measurement of its societal effect to a new level of inclusivity, because it sees societal effects as directly connected with its business model. Justice42 ("Justice for Two," also known as J42) is a dispute-resolution platform that's helping people navigate one of the most challenging experiences in life—divorce. The company mediates divorces via the internet, while empowering separating couples to make a viable arrangement with each other outside of a courtroom. Couples are supported by a professional mediator and receive a divorce certificate signed by a Dutch family judge.

Justice42 uses the **social return on investment (SROI) method** to assess its impact. SROI is based on set principles of measuring the environmental or social effects of a company, the so-called "extra-financial value." The method is based on as-is analysis and describes the effects of a company's intervention over time. The core principles of this method were defined by Social Value International and Social Value UK, and include the following points:[9]

- Involve stakeholders.
- Understand what changes.
- Value the things that matter.
- Only include what is material.
- Do not over-claim.
- Be transparent.
- Verify the result.

The SROI calculation results in a ratio that describes the social return on every dollar invested.

Accordingly, the outcomes of Justice42's service can be measured in the social and emotional well-being of parents and their children. Another benefit could be the substantial amount of money the process saves the Dutch government, which then can be used for other causes. The public now has an alternative to expensive divorce attorneys and court costs, and Justice42 has determined that its investment of one Euro results in a three-Euro return for society.

Every manager within Justice42 is focused on sustaining and even improving this ROI and these outcomes through better service and scale.

IOOI and SROI are not the only methods for measuring and documenting your social impact, yet they are the ones we have encountered most regularly in our work with companies exploring the social impact of their work. One of the struggles in differentiating between these approaches is their similarity, in that both IOOI and SROI initially derive their measurement from the concrete problem they want to solve. The breaking down of the SROI to a concrete number is a first step to comparability of impact.

A couple of other examples will give a glimpse into how a network of companies have developed more elaborate, sometimes even comparative, systems of measuring impact.

The London Benchmarking Group (LBG) is a network of companies that have used the IOOI method to create a more comparative understanding of the impact of larger corporations. The B Corp movement provides the B Impact Assessment, an instrument that looks at a company's impact on its employees, the environment, the community, and its customers.[10] The Common Good Balance Sheet from Economy for a Common Good tries to do something similar.[11] The Sustainability Accounting Standards Board in the US is trying to establish a measurement standard similar to how the accounting profession measures the financials of a company.[12] The Value Balancing Alliance, founded by eight large corporations, is developing new methods of impact measurement and valuation to set a standard for corporations.[13]

While we've seen many reasons why better understanding the societal impact of a company is important, measuring the social impact of healthy lifestyle education, energy poverty, coding education, drinking water distribution systems, to name a few, is nevertheless dependent on context and will stay complex for a while.

However, the growing abundance of data in these fields will make it increasingly easy to demonstrate the effects of a company's community engagement. By the way, it is just as valuable in this work to talk about failures as about successes. Learning from failures may sometimes be of even higher value for a society, since those examples may prevent the investment of public money in solutions already shown to have little or no societal effect.

THE TRUTH ABOUT MEASUREMENT

The issue of measurement can keep a person up at night. Every other day, it seems, we are asked to describe the impact of a school program, a youth program, a tree-planting project, or a corporate-purpose program. Companies look for a simple answer, a quick and clear way to document their social-good efforts for their board, shareholders, regulators, required reports, and society. Ideally, they want the one indicator that will illustrate the shift of a whole community, region, or society arising from one donation, program, or intervention. This one indicator may never exist. We have to pursue measurement and accept its limitations. Maybe it is this tension that, in the end, will help us to improve the impact of the engagement for society.

The truth is that a solution is most often the result of many people and organizations addressing an issue simultaneously and over time.

While we understand this desire, we also know a simple answer is impossible. The world is complex, and achieving change in our education system, the environment, household poverty levels, or any other social cause is extraordinarily difficult. As professionals, we'd love to be able to say, "This *one* intervention from a company solved a concrete problem." The truth is that a solution is most often the result of many people and organizations addressing an issue simultaneously and over time.

For example, an organization may want a simple measurement of its impact on the education of children: namely, the number of children served. But an education intervention is complex and affects others far beyond just the student, including teachers, volunteers, parents, partnerships, the community, and the education system as a whole. To capture a truly realistic view, the organization would need to measure and reflect on its impact on all these groups.

This chapter encourages you to measure your impact. It's only fair to warn you that this can be a long journey and a walk on the narrow line between pragmatism and scientific rigor.

Yet, it's worth walking this line every time.

TRAIT 7:
Design and Innovation Questions

When managing with a corporate social mind, you should always ask yourself the following questions:

- What do we want to achieve for the community and for our company with our societal engagement?
- How can we break down our strategy in an IOOI theory-of-change model?
- How can we use our capacities of measuring core business data, reputation, efficiency, etc., for this task?
- What stories of change do we want to capture (qualitative data) and what numbers do we want to track (quantitative data)?
- How do we need and want to report to the public on our community work?
- How do we want to share what we learn with each other and the public?

We come back to Einstein: "Not everything that counts can be counted, and not everything that can be counted counts." You must always question the usefulness of the information gathered for you as a manager and for society.[14] Sometimes the impact is so obvious that you do not need to measure it, sometimes what you measure says nothing about your impact, and sometimes things may be so experimental that it makes sense to actually evaluate the impact of the intervention. Measuring your impact is crucial for the corporate social mind, but it is not the solution to all means, and it does not always describe actual impact.

INTERVIEW

Laura Kistemaker,
Uitelkaar & Justice42 (Justice for Two)

"A company is the most sustainable way to engage in a social issue . . . [because] the solution itself can generate the funds, and the existential reason to continue is proven."

LAURA KISTEMAKER, co-founder and COO of Dutch start-up Uitelkaar & J42 (Justice42), believes that highly influential companies take a risk when they don't get involved in social good. She explains how crucial social impact measurement has become for her team in improving the company's credibility and performance. You'll see how she has turned a social issue into a component of the company's service that's as vital as any other.

Michael: Please describe your role at Uitelkaar & Justice42 or Justice for Two.

Laura: I'm co-founder and COO of Uitelkaar & Justice42, which is our company name, and we've built an online divorce platform that is not only for married couples wishing to divorce, but also for couples who've been together, have children together, but decide to separate. It's an online platform that basically guides couples through their divorce in a de-escalating way.

Both the system and the people around the system—our case managers and the mediators who work with us—support them or offer guidance when needed. So, it's a blended online process, and it really puts users in the driver's seat of drafting divorce and parenting agreements.

Michael: Was there a social vision behind the company from the beginning?

Laura: Yes, absolutely. It really started out with the social mission to improve the divorce process that in many countries, including the Netherlands, causes a lot of negative impact on the couple, but especially on the children. It also costs society a lot of money, and so the idea was that technology could be used to empower people to make better agreements. It's very important still today for us. It's really ingrained in the design of the product and of the service.

Michael: What personal values drive you, and how do these personal values intersect with Uitelkaar & Justice42?

Laura: I've always been a person who loves to work hard to get results. I love it when the issue is complex, but my reward is not so much in earning heaps of money or getting status. I need to get my reward from something else, which really pushes me and drives me in my daily work: It has to have meaning for people who are in some of the worst places in their lives; and that I, in some way, can contribute to making it a bit less difficult for them, or at least to making the future a bit better for them. That's what makes me absolutely love what I do.

Michael: How do you measure your societal impact, and why is that important to you?

Laura: It's important to us for a number of reasons, because it guides our strategic decisions, it helps us communicate what we do, and the way we measure helps us focus. So, we want a measurement tool that, in a very smart way, measures the effect of using our tool on the couples, on the lawyers and mediators that work with us, and also on the legal aid board in the Netherlands, which is responsible for financing a large part of the cost of divorce for people with low incomes.

We measure mainly by surveying our customers at different points of the process so we can also measure how they change during the course of being on a platform. The length of the interaction of the user with our platform is quite long—from three months to more than a year. We measure the well-being of the people involved, and we measure the quality of parent-child relations over time. For lawyers and mediators, we can measure hard financial benefits, but we're also interested in their job satisfaction, because our system helps them with administrative issues. They can spend more time where they can really add value. This brings us sometimes very surprising insights.

Michael: Can you give an example?

Laura: In one of the last surveys, our lawyers and mediators started telling us they like the kind of clients they get through us. They get cases where people are sensible, they have thought through want they want, and they're respectful of each other. It's a job satisfaction aspect that we didn't think of.

Michael: You work a lot with government agencies and the like. Was it important to present your impact case when you started to scale the service?

Laura: Yes, especially because the divorce process is closely tied to the administrative procedure of government, and there's kind of a hesitation to work with private entities. The fact that we are not so much a commercial entity, but still a company with a social mission, helps us a lot in explaining to the government what our intentions are.

Michael: You are partly owned by a foundation, aren't you?

Laura: Yes. We are part owned by a foundation. Impact investors are backing us, and then we can make visible what we do. It's not just a narrative that we can present. It's also the numbers behind the narrative, which our government needs for us to be accountable. That's also very useful in our communications.

Michael: Does the social mission focus of your company have an impact on the culture of your company and your employees?

Laura: I definitely think that it attracts a certain type of employee. A lot of applicants say they want to be part of something that results in a bit more than selling another product of some sort, especially with the younger generations. We're very close to our customers because our case managers, our contact center, are in touch with them every day. We know who the beneficiaries of our service are, and we get that feedback. It trickles down to everything. For example, we would not market our product in a cheap and dirty way because that would not fit who we are and who we want to be—even if it would be the way to attract the most divorce cases.

> *". . . don't be naive about all the challenges you'll face. You'd better make sure you're extremely passionate about what you do because you'll need that energy to keep going."*

Michael: Out of your experience, what advice would you give to companies about tackling social issues?

Laura: If you're a company with a lot of influence, your social mission might be on the bottom of your priority list. I think that's a risk. If you really want to tackle social issues, it needs to be inseparable from the products or service you offer.

And don't underestimate the complexity of the social issues environment—don't be naive about all the challenges you'll face. You'd better make sure you're extremely passionate about what you do because you'll need that energy to keep going. Which is logical, because if the social issue you're trying to solve was easy to tackle, it would have been done already.

My advice would be don't be discouraged if you meet resistance. It's often an environment where a lot of vested interests have been active for a long, long time. If your product or service or offering makes sense, if its essence is good, you'll get there, but you'll need the energy and the passion to keep going.

Michael: Sounds like it's a marathon!

Laura: It is a marathon, but one you do with a lot of people at once. I'd also say, please invest in your stakeholders. You really need ambassadors in different places that believe in your cause and are willing to tell your story, open doors, help with the work, or make you see things that you didn't see yourself. Although it may not bring you money or a new customer immediately, please spend time on shaping those relationships.

Michael: In your business, you collaborate with lawyers, mediators, judges, and the government. That's a lot of collaborators to manage.

Laura: With so many players, collaboration is key. Making friends in the field is key, but also don't be afraid to say things that might shake up the vested interests because things need to change in order to bring the solution a bit closer.

Michael: Was there a management principle or tools that helped you focus on your social issues?

Laura: I don't know whether it's a management principle, but one thing I learned is that having a multidisciplinary team is key because you're playing two games. You're playing the commercial game as a company that needs to stay alive financially, and you're playing the social impact game. Doing just one of those things is already pretty hard for everyone, so to do both, you really need different people with different skills.

In business, it always feels safer to work with people who have a similar background to yours with the same skill sets who understand your language. But especially in the social enterprise arena, that's not what you need. You need different people with different backgrounds who can complement each other, because it's basically two different entities in one.

Another principle that I really believe in is transparency and openness—internally in the team, as well as to the outside world. Letting people see why you do what you do. Don't be afraid to show when you decided on something that didn't work—especially for the team. They join something and don't necessarily know how things will turn out. Therefore, be transparent about what you're doing and how you're doing it.

Michael: What for you is the most important argument for doing this initiative with a company, rather than with an NGO or within a government agency or some other way?

Laura: In the end, a company is the most sustainable way to engage in a social issue. Previously, this project was financed by the government, which brought a lot of benefits, but also became a huge existential disadvantage: If people give you money, they can also take it away from you. With a change of leadership or policy that you cannot influence, all the work that so many people have put into your project is lost.

If you manage to make a company out of your solution, then the solution itself can generate the funds, and the existential reason to continue is proven. I wouldn't say it's the easiest way, and I also know the numbers of failing social enterprises, but I think that when you manage it for the long term, a company is definitely the best solution.

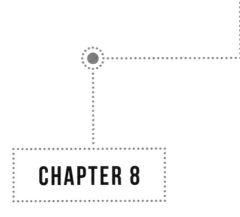

CHAPTER 8

Trait 8: A Corporate Social Mind
Innovates for Social Good

All innovations address both a business need and a social need. The company always applies its services, knowledge, and consumer insights to creating or enhancing something that benefits both itself and society.

Innovation is an important driver of all aspects of life. Business in particular is a player very much dependent on introducing new ideas, products, and services that react to changing consumer expectations or environmental changes. Thus, innovation is crucial for business performance. Many of these innovations impact society; some contribute to solving certain problems, while some create new or aggravate existing problems.

The corporate social mind looks at any innovation with society in mind. It more purposefully drives innovation processes that will contribute to solving big and small challenges humanity faces today.

FOCUS

This chapter will be a short expedition into the practice of social innovation within companies and will explore the following questions:

- What is social innovation?
- How can we make social questions relevant for innovations?
- How can we identify our team's potential for social innovations?

TRAIT 8 IN ACTION

Germany's Ruhr Valley has undergone an economic transformation away from its long dependency on the steel and coal industries. In the southeast corner of this once-industrial heartland lies Witten, a city of 96,000 that today has shifted to a diverse array of economic clusters: mechanical engineering, chemical production, digital technology, medicine, and related services. In this ecosystem, social and business innovations seem to cross, merge, and evolve.

If you travel by train into Witten, as most people do, you can sense the struggle behind the economic metamorphosis. Empty stores line its main shopping road, while those that are open advertise "One Euro" deals. Nevertheless, the city boasts the charm of houses from various time periods, the cultural diversity of its inhabitants, and the often rough-but-friendly way of its citizens.

Witten may seem an odd place to explore one of the most crucial traits of the corporate social mind—the need to combine business and social needs in any innovation. In reality, though, this small town is one of the better examples for understanding the definition of social innovation and the global thirst for it.

SMALL BUSINESS, BIG IMPACT: DR. AUSBÜTTEL & CO. GMBH

Dr. Ausbüttel & Co. GmbH has been a family-owned healthcare business in Witten since 1894. Headquartered in an area of shopping and residential use, the 130-employee company produces wound, eye, and pain care products.

An aura of innovation is palpable with your first step onto the campus—an assemblage of containers and buildings looking as if someone played with LEGO bricks in a big way.[1] Inside, although it's buzzing with activity, every employee offers a friendly greeting, and you'll notice more workers with physical challenges than at most other businesses you have visited.

Stephan Kohorst, the third-generation CEO, explains in the interview after chapter 2 how innovation, inclusion, and social impact go hand in hand in this dynamic company. From its start in a local pharmacy, Dr. Ausbüttel & Co. GmbH has evolved into an innovation machine.

One key to this innovator's success is being an active part of the local community and learning about challenges faced by people who are physically and mentally disadvantaged. Beyond employing so many people with disabilities in the main campus (and up to 1,100 more working at packaging sites), the company extends its social impact by ensuring every innovation meets both a business need and a social need. And, under construction at this printing, its new headquarters has been intentionally designed to allow more inclusivity and job opportunities for people from all walks of life and with all sorts of challenges.

The public probably won't read about Dr. Ausbüttel & Co. as an example of corporate social innovation, like Unilever or Danone, but they should. The company shows how values, entrepreneurship, and closeness to the community can create a small ecosystem that drives improvements in business and community through a single innovation when it's viewed through a social lens.

SMALL BUSINESS, BIG IMPACT: PROJEKTFABRIK/JOBACT®

Another social innovation company on Witten's main shopping street has turned its work into a global lever for change. Projektfabrik has garnered acclaim in Scandinavia, Spain, South Korea, and other parts of the world for using artistic expression to address systemic social and economic bottlenecks. One such service, JobAct*, helps people under 30 discover their potential and find their place in life—especially their work life.

Founder Sandra Schürmann has done what innovation researchers consider one of the key drivers of innovation today. She created something brand-new by combining two services (or interventions) for the very first time. She brought theatre pedagogy together with her extensive experience working with unemployed youth in the Ruhr Valley to help participants build self-esteem, discover what true teamwork looks like, and learn skills to find a job they'll enjoy.

Here's how it works: Over six months, young people write, design, promote, and perform a play, some in prominent theatre houses. Here's what it does: After the program, the chances of a participant either getting a job or going back to school are twice as high as in most comparable programs. Projektfabrik and Schürmann have received countless awards, including a €4 million grant from the JPMorgan Chase Foundation. A grant of this size by a corporate foundation was previously unheard of for a German social enterprise.

ADJUST THE BUSINESS LENS

The drive for innovation makes sense outside of business, yet we continue to talk about innovation and disruption through a business lens. Meanwhile, the Social Innovation Exchange in London is promoting applied social innovation to seek solutions for manifold societal problems around the world. Apolitical in London is among those doing the same for the government sector. And far-reaching innovations in drones, nanotechnology, blockchain technology, and how we ensure our well-being are changing the way we live together, and they hold potential for solving societal and environmental challenges a company might not consider when developing an innovation.

Many examples show that human interaction can be the starting point for innovation, yet so can current technology. Consider the way start-up companies, both for-profit and not-for-profit, are using blockchain technology (a way to store and secure digital entries like in a ledger) to bring traceability and transparency to industries:

- When online clothier Zalando joined the Dutch accelerator Fashion for Good, their joint accelerator had a focus on how blockchain technology could lead to social good in the textile industry. In this innovation process, Zalando shares its logistics and industry knowledge with the sector and provides scale to innovative start-ups focused on sustainability and transparency.

- KARUNA, a social cooperative in Berlin, partnered with Google.org to develop the MOKLI Helpfinder app, bringing transparency about services for homeless youth by helping them locate nearby services. Since then, MOKLI has developed a blockchain solution that revolutionizes the way those who are homeless access services and resources: Charities and donors can designate gifts for specific needs (meals, overnight shelter, etc.) that users can redeem through a digital wallet without needing their own bank account.

The MOKLI initiative is a good illustration of what can happen when leaders of a large company like Google think about their corporate skills as resources for society. *It is a mindset—one for all business leaders to adopt.* Such a mindset is a game-changer for social good and good business; though an innovative idea may result in a zero on the balance sheet, it may deliver a satisfying social ROI.

Some of these innovations may have low initial margins and resemble investments that we hope pay off in the distant future. Innovation applied to residential construction to create cheaper houses or micro-houses for low-income families is a good example. Viewing these innovations with a corporate social mindset opens you to valuing social inclusion and cohesion. You then might see that shared benefits and "free rides" could ensure the stability of a community, allowing low-wage earners to become consumers and local-business customers.

SOCIAL ISSUES DRIVE BUSINESS RELEVANCY

Many business/social-good partnerships already exist. Yet, it is surprising to many entrepreneurs that business leaders who talk about these collaborations don't tend to mention the philanthropic aspect first. Instead, they state unequivocally that companies must venture into the social sector to stay relevant, innovative, and challenged.

For instance, sustainability demands from consumers were the motivation to improve supply chains in cacao and palm oil. Caring for older adults and those with disabilities could become another, with autonomous driving potentially opening the door to innumerable options for people who cannot drive a car. Yes, these and so many more issues are both societal challenges and business opportunities. Innovating to find solutions will allow you to stay in business.

We anticipate some skepticism in the form of "Isn't this just the perception of do-gooders who have fallen for a company's hype? These were all simply business opportunities the public just didn't understand."

Some companies justify the skepticism, of course. But we encourage you to think about businesses as being strongly connected to the social and environmental challenges of our planet. This—and the entrepreneur's or manager's values—should be the drivers of businesses.

Examples of values-driven businesses may not always be obvious, such as US carpet tile producer Interface, Inc., which will eliminate any negative environmental impact by 2020, or German home appliances producer Vorwerk, which cut its CO_2 emissions by half from 2016 to 2018 and is pursuing a zero environmental impact strategy. Still, our research shows again and again that owners and managers of businesses consider innovation driven by values and social engagement as part of their DNA. In today's world, it should be no surprise that the same is true for a growing number of publicly traded companies.

Though not occurring with lightning speed, this mindset shift is becoming integrated into the policy frameworks of national governments and multilateral organizations. The Canadian government has introduced a national Social Innovation and Social Finance Strategy. The European Union has begun a policy of funding social innovation and has built a portal to extensive resources and knowledge. In many other examples around the world, companies are inviting the not-for-profit sector to collaborate, and vice versa. By providing a good overview of such initiatives, the Social Innovation Index (created by the Economist Intelligence Unit), which measures and ranks the capacity of 45 countries to drive social innovation, should make it even easier for companies to expand their scope of (social) innovation.

A MATTER OF COMFORT

Social innovation is also the space in which philanthropy, government, and business seem to feel most comfortable in exploring partnerships. XPRIZE and the initiatives for innovative solutions in healthcare and personal hygiene from the Bill & Melinda Gates Foundation are examples. The Action Tank initiative in France and similar initiatives in Portugal, Belgium, and the Netherlands bring companies together to explore how they can contribute to poverty reduction and social cohesion. Action Tank produced a list of amazing examples of companies achieving social impact while enhancing business—such as Renault's Garage Solidaire, which gives single mothers at-cost access to the repair shops of more than 3,000 partners. By restoring their vehicles to working condition at a lower cost, this innovation enables mothers to keep their jobs and families intact.

François Rouvier (Expert Leader for Social Business at Renault) shows in the interview after this chapter how Renault successfully leveraged the expertise of the company and its partners in a way no one thought possible, establishing partnerships with and among civil society and government to ensure their program reaches those who need it most. Some of our colleagues call this "collective impact" or "networked solutions." These may be new words for something that has always made sense in human development: collaborate, communicate, and create together.

The list of societal challenges that need innovative approaches to solutions seems to be unending. The 17 Sustainable Development Goals set by the United Nations in 2015 create a good compass for these challenges. The SDGs start with the fight against poverty, encompass quality education and responsible consumption and production, and end with the formation of partnerships to reach these goals. The SDGs describe challenges we face in every part of the world, and companies around the globe are using them as a framework for their innovations.

REASSESS BUSINESS FOR UNSEEN POTENTIAL

Now is the time for companies to consider how their existing innovations can be applied to societal challenges, as Renault did. In this process, remember to bring your new two-pronged mindset to innovation: How can I use my resources for society, and what societal challenges could drive my own business innovation?

Such a reassessment doesn't have to add substantially to anyone's current workload. We have found that it's more like a re-exploration of your company than a new project.

Social innovation is much like any other innovation cycle you know, with two main differences: First, a corporate social mindset allows you to introduce a societal demand into the process on a much stronger footing. Second, some of the barriers to implementing this kind of thinking and action may be unusual to business leaders.

POTENTIAL BARRIERS TO SOCIAL INNOVATION

You may encounter barriers such as those that follow:

- *Management's lack of willingness to cooperate:* To develop solutions, you will have to rely on previously unfamiliar partners, such as nonprofit organizations. This will increase your uncertainty and risk, but don't let it make you unwilling to work with others.

- *Complexity of the problem:* Social challenges are complex. They are not just about money, but encompass the societal environment, education, and many other factors with implications for product/service design and marketing. Coordination and regulation are also complex, with no established framework or advocates for social innovations in the corporate environment.

- *Lack of awareness:* The general lack of awareness of the challenges faced by some members of the population means fewer people (e.g., market researchers and analysts) have thought about suitable services or the purchasing behavior of people who face hardship.

If the values and resources of a company are the neurons of a corporate social mindset, then innovations are the neurotransmitters flying across synapses and creating real buzz in the mind.

A retailer once got in touch with us to ask how it could explore the ecosystem of start-ups with a social mission. Although the company had a tremendous innovation culture, its management felt it was missing out on something and could challenge itself to do better, knowing that some innovations must come from external sources. Thus, it saw these start-ups as places where innovation and the social mind were operating hand in hand. The company believed it could study these start-ups to enhance its own innovation capabilities while learning to better understand social issues.

This inquiry began a journey into a world of social innovations that, until then, had been foreign to the company.

This approach opened up amazing conversations among certain global corporate social innovators. Besides agility and some of the other traits we associate with the culture of (social) start-ups, technological and service innovations were introduced as topics of exploration. The process is ongoing. We'll watch to see how the long-term ideas and products developed with social change in mind will change the way this company works.

It's exciting when we can initiate these kinds of cross-sector discussions and processes. It's clear that social innovations by business will provide answers to some of the toughest societal problems today—and a corporate social mindset is absolutely necessary for this.

TRAIT 8:
Design and Innovation Questions

The following can serve as your business and social innovation checklist:

- **Corporate Asset Scan:** What are our company's capacities? How could these assets contribute (even more than they are already) to solving problems our societies face? We have seen that the sophisticated use of corporate data is extremely helpful here; it may indicate or suggest relationships between the company and certain groups in need.

- **Community Relations Map:** What are our connections to the local community regionally, nationally, and globally? Besides our usual supply partners, customers also look closely at the way we give, provide pro bono support, and act generously in other ways.

- **Understanding the Issue:** What are the actual challenges vulnerable communities face? What do we need to know about the issue and the people that face it? Understanding these issues is crucial to determining which of your business applications, communications, and marketing resources you could innovate for a cause.

- **Prototype:** What could a prototype of an innovation look like? Such a model often can be done with people on the team that have managed community relations and corporate citizenship and have established ties to the community.

Are you ready to overcome these barriers with your drive for innovation? Only people and companies willing to think innovatively about business resources as assets for society will solve today's formidable social and environmental challenges at home and abroad and advance their business.

INTERVIEW

François Rouvier, Renault

"Once companies understand that government can't do any-thing more and that the responsibility for alleviating poverty is in the hands of companies, I think things will change."

FRANÇOIS ROUVIER, Expert Leader Social Business at Renault, explains how the carmaker has made a concise effort to understand social exclusion in France and has developed a social innovation with social impact that evolved into a business case. You'll hear how the mobility of people inside a vehicle naturally led to a concern for their mobility outside of one and how the company applied its social-good philosophy throughout its operations.

Michael: Can you describe your role at Renault and how you are engaged with lead and design, social impact, and sustainability work at the company?

François: I'm in charge of the social business, or inclusive business project, in Renault, which was born within the corporate social responsibility direction in Renault. We had decided to launch this experiment in 2011 to implement the idea of social business that we have started to develop into design.

> *"If everyone had more altruism and generosity,*
> *the world and the society could be much better,*
> *much richer, for everybody."*

Michael: What personal values drive you, and how do they intersect with the work of Renault?

François: My first value is really a point of interest: Humanism, I would say. I am very deeply focused on altruism and generosity. I believe strongly that the world should be better. If everyone had more altruism and generosity, the world and the society could be much better, much richer, for everybody. As far as my job is concerned, I try to connect the two. That's why I see social business as a kind of synthesis.

Michael: What is the focus of Renault when it comes to social impact and sustainability work?

François: Renault definitely used to be a car manufacturer and is becoming, as all car manufacturers are, a mobility service provider. It means we are definitely trying now not only to make or design cars, but are now moving to be a company that tries to propose a range of services connected to mobility first.

Second, for quite a long time, we've been a very popular company—not a premium brand like BMW or Mercedes Benz. We are really a folk brand, and so Renault is very close to people. I take "mobility for all" as the hub of what Renault is. As a mobility provider, as a service mobility provider, it was quite natural that we proposed to expand "mobility for all" to be mobility for those who in reality have no mobility at all or no more access to mobility. The social business was very connected to the DNA of Renault.

Michael: Can you share the basic idea of Mobilize? Why do you say it is creating access for people that may not have mobility right now?

François: Mobilize was the name of this idea: to try to do business with people at the bottom of the pyramid, people who are no longer customers of Renault because they cannot afford a brand-new Renault or even a recent secondhand Renault. The only car they can afford is a very, very old one they buy on websites, where they take the risk of losing everything. These are the people we are targeting, those people for whom mobility is critical to finding and keeping a job, but who no longer have the financial capacity to maintain or purchase those cars.

Then within Mobilize, we have several initiatives—for example, Garage Solidaire, the repair and maintenance side of the program. Let's say you're in a difficult situation financially and you need to get your car repaired to get a job. A state or governmental organization will connect you to a Renault Garage Solidaire close to your home, and from that time on, no one makes any profit: the garage, the mechanic, the parts dealer, Renault, no one. This cuts the total invoice by roughly 50%. If the car can't be repaired and you're eligible—and most people are—we'll find a way to get them a new car for around 60 to 80 Euros per month.

Michael: Is your core partner always government, or do you also work with welfare organizations?

François: We work with several kinds of welfare organizations, including some private ones, but most are connected to the government.

Michael: How would you describe the effect of Mobilize overall on the company and its employees?

François: First, I'm sure it's a motivating factor for employees. Those who know the program are quite proud of the fact that Renault exerts their responsibility, their social responsibility, and tries to make the situation better for poor people.

Second, we have demonstrated since 2011 that social business has driven innovations. We have the right to take much bigger risks, so we can experiment.

Third, we have contributed to make entrepreneurship more popular. We have created a contest of entrepreneurial projects within the company, and this is becoming very, very popular.

Finally, employees today want to be more engaged at work, and the way to be engaged is really to support the projects they do. I think we offer the chance for people to be engaged through our own projects or even by finding new ideas and being more creative.

Michael: Was there a specific moment in your career when you decided you wanted to do this for Renault instead of staying in traditional business development?

François: Yes, a very personal something happened in my life. It was in 2002 when I got cancer. For eight months, I had to stop working or do limited work from home when I wasn't completely out for chemotherapy. I had time to think over my future. I was quite young, about 35, 36 years old. I said to myself that something had to change, I had to be more centered. When I heard about social business, I said to myself, "That's really what I want to do."

Michael: Given your experience with Renault, what are some basic ideas for how a company should tackle a social issue?

François: I think first, for the one who is the entrepreneur, it's necessary to have the experience of the company. To have a network. You cannot do it alone by arriving alone in the company. When I started this in 2010–11, I had a network, an internal network. I had the credibility within the company.

Once you have this prerequisite, I think it's a little bit like marketing, normal marketing. Customers from the bottom of the pyramid are people, and you have to understand well their needs and how you can match them with your products or services.

We didn't invent Garage Solidaire, but we did our research and decided we could do it better and on a larger scale with our own network. When you decide to offer some social business, you don't have to replicate. You have to be pragmatic.

In the case of social business, you co-build, you co-construct, you co-invent. It's important to be embedded into an ecosystem to understand with whom we could connect. Then you can find solutions absolutely everywhere.

Every time people are dedicated and every time people really want it, we find solutions. Even in B2B you can invent social businesses.

Michael: Are there certain management principles or tools that have been especially helpful?

François: A key word is trust. Creating confidence. As a big company, you're looked at with suspicion by potential partners and customers, so it's fundamental to create confidence and trust with them. It's the same with your internal audiences because you are proposing something disrupting to your company. You have to apply the same management rules as the one you apply when you are a good manager: You must be very accurate and rigorous, very strict on budget management.

Michael: What is the one most important argument for a company to do what you and Renault have done?

François: We have no choice. It's so easy to talk about corporate social responsibility just for the purpose of communication. That's totally crazy. If you just do it for communication, you have not understood the scope and the importance of your responsibility. Companies are responsible for the environment. It's the same for social responsibility. Once companies understand that government can't do anything more and that the responsibility for alleviating poverty is in the hands of companies, I think things will change. When they understand that their engagement contributes to a better place for them to exist and a better feeling for their employees, I'm sure they will engage more.

Business Value and Social Value
as One Philosophy

Something is changing in the world of business and societies overall. It is an evolving understanding that we must address the problems of the world we live in. It is an understanding that these problems, from social inclusion to climate, are all connected to each other and the purpose of what we do.

This book is based on the need for companies to expand their understanding of the assets they have to contribute to addressing societal issues. The stories and examples in this book demonstrate how companies that integrate their community and social involvement step by step into the core of their work and purpose create a different and better societal impact. Within a business, this means that marketing, sustainability, innovation, supply chain, controlling, finance, development, sales, production, communication, and corporate social responsibility have to integrate their expertise and experience. An integrated approach asks you to overcome thinking and acting in silos.

It's a given these days that effective leadership is crucial to managing a successful business. This is even more true with the business' societal responsibility in mind. Many have written about managing in a world of growing complexity. *The Corporate Social Mind* asks you not only to face this complexity, but to seize it as an opportunity for business to improve society.

In the end, the corporate social mind is about the way you think, the way you express your values and opinions—a true mindset.

We have to remember, though, that the work we do on social issues is a marathon, not a sprint. It involves consistent learning, discovery, and iteration to ensure that every moment passes a certain milestone for the issue and your target audiences. In essence, a new mindset takes time, and progress on social issues is an effort with meaningful, long-term outcomes.

This book introduced leaders in business who have challenged themselves and the companies they own, lead, or work for to take on social issues for more than just the good of the business. They are reinventing—some may claim rediscovering—the purpose of business and, in most if not all cases, their own purpose, too.

But we also understand that every business needs to walk a fine line when it comes to their social issue engagement. Approaches to social issues often breed new situations in which choices may result in undesired outcomes. Just consider the recent debate and the outcome of Nike's stand against racial injustice with the American football player Colin Kaepernick and how it conflicted with other practices of the company, such as how women athletes are not paid as much as their male counterparts.[1] Even just assessing the social and environmental effects of a product or service may force many businesses to confront such difficult decisions.

Even with all the enthusiasm we have for the corporate social mind (and it is great), we are aware that it presents dilemmas. These dilemmas start with the perception of the overall role of business in our societies. It is not a surprise that phrases like "green washing" (misleading claims on environmental impact and work by a company about a practice, service, or product) or "white washing" (glossing over or not addressing major issues, challenges, or problematic practices) are often brought up by critics when discussing the societal engagement of companies. But businesses these days know very well that authenticity and trust are corporate values in themselves. Furthermore, business and society need to persevere through the tension and discover the reason why the overall purpose of a business is such an important topic today.

Another argument we often are confronted with is the so-called "free rider effect."[2] It's true that other businesses may profit from you taking responsibility for a societal issue or driving a social innovation. But that's no reason not to pursue social initiatives. It all comes down to having the courage to take responsibility in business. We've shown, through the stories in this book, how good business management and the corporate social mind coming together can create substantial societal and business value. The CEO of Sympatex shows us how a radical belief in an environment-first model can disrupt a whole industry. Renault shows that the courage to better understanding the reasons for social exclusion at your own front door can create both tremendous social impact *and* profitability.

A quote by H. Jackson Brown's mother (and usually misattributed to Mark Twain) may say it best: "Twenty years from now, you will be more disappointed by the things you didn't do than by the ones you did do. So throw off the bowlines. Sail away from the safe harbor. Catch the trade winds in your sails. Explore. Dream. Discover."

Corporate social issue involvement is a journey that requires a particular mindset for success. *The Corporate Social Mind* invites you to cast off.

ACKNOWLEDGMENTS

FOREMOST IN DERRICK'S MIND . . .

- are INFLUENCE|SG team members Cassie Evard and Dr. Amy Thayer for their devotion, time, and expertise.

- are the Ad Council team, including Lisa Sherman, Barbara Leshinsky, Kate Emanuel, Megan Sigesmund, Colleen Thompson-Kuhn, and Ken Kroll. Thank you. You have been instrumental in creating change with companies through marketing and communications while allowing me to help explore new opportunities that are leading to new discoveries.

- are the many people that inspire and challenge my own thinking. A special thank you to Tony Foleno, Senior Vice President of Strategy and Evaluation of the Ad Council, Asha Curran, Executive Director of GivingTuesday, Jean Case, CEO of the Case Foundation, Clay Robbins, CEO of Lilly Endowment,

Simon Moss, Co-Founder of Global Citizen, Charmian Love, Chair and Co-Founder of B Lab UK, and Kathy Buechel with The Benter Foundation.

FOREMOST IN MICHAEL'S MIND . . .

- are current and former Wider Sense members, including Theresa Bartsch, Lisa Born, Lea Buck, Nadine Bubner, Britta Engling, Maximilian Grimm, Kerstin Ischen, Anne Marie Jacob, Simon Kaiser, Anne-Sophie Oehrlein, Julia Oestreich, Carmen Pägelow, Eva Schneider, Gabriele Störmann, Fabian Suwanprateep, Anna Wolf, and Michael's current business partner, Stephan Dorgerloh. A special thank you to Dr. Felicitas Peter! Each of these individuals has been at the forefront of discovery and strategy—inspiring truly global impact. Thanks also to Dr. Stephan Goetz and Stefan Sankjohanser, the founders and owners of goetzpartners, who have been crucial in creating an enabling environment for me to gain the experience and knowledge that is the basis for this book. Armin Raffalski has been an amazing companion on this path, as have many other members of the goetzpartners team.

- are the many people who challenge my work and are always open for reflection about our experiences. A special thank you to Prof. Dr. Laura Marie Edinger-Schons, Chair of Corporate Social Responsibility at the University of Mannheim, Dr. Holger Backhaus-Maul from the Martin Luther University in

Halle-Wittenberg, and Dr. Knut Bergmann, Head of Communication and the Branch Office in Berlin of the German Economic Institute. A special thank you also goes to Felix Dresewski, Director of the Kurt and Maria Dohle Foundation, who as a friend and colleague always challenges the status quo.

FOREMOST IN BOTH OUR MINDS . . .

- are the people who inspired and supported us in bringing this idea and book to life.

- are the wonderful people who made this book possible: Cindy Dashnaw, Tyler Hansen, and the team at Greenleaf Book Group. In addition, we must thank the individuals who made time in their busy schedules to allow us to spend time with them to help others see social-issue engagement differently: Koen Demaesschalck, Rüdiger Fox, Jennifer Foyle, Karin Heyl, Christiane Hoelscher, Laura Kistemaker, Stephan Kohorst, Daniel Lee, Christine McGrath, David Raper, François Rouvier, Tom Sazky, and Dr. Nathalie von Siemens.

- are the people we work with every day who remind us of the reason we do the work we do for social change.

- is the Bertelsmann Foundation and The McConnell Foundation that brought us together and allowed us to collaborate on projects. These projects always provided good moments for us to further our own thinking.

- are the many clients that allowed us to gain experiences together with them and create social impact every day.

THANK YOU ALL.

NOTES

....

INTRODUCTION

1. "From Good Intentions to Good Results: Corporate Citizenship of Germany's DAX 30 Companies," Wider Sense and goetzpartners (May 2017), https://en.widersense.org/studies/corporate-citizenship-benchmark.

CHAPTER 1

1. Adam Smith, *The Theory of Moral Sentiments*. London: Printed for A. Millar, and A. Kincaid and J. Bell: Edinburgh, 1759.

2. Chris D. Frith and Tania Singer, "The role of social cognition in decision making," *Philosophical Transactions of the Royal Society B*. 363 (October 2008): https://doi.org/10.1098/rstb.2008.0156.

3. Siemens, "Business to Society Report: Making Real What Matters to the USA," 2017, https://assets.new.siemens.com/siemens/assets/api/uuid:6ca41768fecba9 46a82b4132b3b667cbc21ffbdc/version:1513279412/ us-cc-b2s-report-120117-en.pdf.

4. "Microsoft's 2018 Annual Report," microsoft.com, accessed January 28, 2020, https://www.microsoft.com/en-us/annualreports/ar2018/annualreport.

CHAPTER 2

1. Salesforce, "About Us"; and CRM 101: "What Is CRM?," salesforce.com, accessed January 28, 2020, https://www.salesforce.com/company/about-us; https://www.salesforce.com/crm/what-is-crm.

2. Robert Safian, "Salesforce's Marc Benioff on the Power of Values," *Fast Company*, April 17, 2017, https://www.fastcompany.com/40397514/salesforces-marc-benioff-on-the-power-of-values.

3. Whole Foods Market, "Company Info," wholefoodsmarket.com, accessed September 6, 2019, www.wholefoodsmarket.com/company-info.

4. American Express, "Supplier Standards and Conduct," americanexpress.com, accessed January 28, 2020, https://www.americanexpress.com/us/supplier-management/supplier-standards/our-blue-box-shared-values.html.

CHAPTER 3

1. About SchlaU-Schule, accessed January 28, 2020, https://www.schlau-schule.de/.

2. Alexander C. Kaufman, "The CEO Who Took on Indiana's Anti-LGBT Law – and Won," April 7, 2015, HuffPost, https://www.huffpost.com/entry/marc-benioff-indiana_n_7017032?guccounter=1.

3. Beyond Philanthropy and Laura Edinger-Schons, *Choosing the right set-up for corporate volunteering: Insights from the DAX30*, University of Mannheim, 2019.

4. Woody Hochswender, "SIGNALS; Why Levi's Don't Fit Scouts," *The New York Times*, May 31, 1992.

CHAPTER 4

1. Bailey Loosemore, "Sorry, we're closed: How everyone is hurt when grocery stores shut down," *Louisville Courier Journal*, January 10, 2019, https://www.courier-journal.com/story/news/local/2019/01/10/louisville-food-deserts-how-grocery-stores-closing-hurt-community/1944809002.

2. Bailey Loosemore, "Kroger's mobile market brings fresh food to Louisville neighborhoods without access," *Louisville Courier Journal*, August 15, 2019, https://www.courier-journal.com/story/news/local/2019/08/15/kroger-launches-mobile-grocery-store-louisville-food-bank/1804469001.

3. Ibid.

4. Ekaterina Petrova, "Why brands should take a stand in their ads: 3 perspectives, 1 campaign," *Think with Google*, November 2017, https://www. thinkwithgoogle.com/advertising-channels/video/pov-cultural-advertising/.

CHAPTER 5

1. Siemens, "Siemens' commitment to refugees," September 14, 2016, https://press.siemens.com/ global/en/feature/siemens-commitment-helping-refugees.

2. Rachel D. Godsil, Linda R. Tropp, Phillip Atiba Goff, and John A. Powell, "Addressing Implicit Bias, Racial Anxiety, and Stereotype Threat in Education and Health Care," *The Science of Equality, Volume 1*, November 2014, http://perception.org/wp-content/ uploads/2014/11/Science-of-Equality-111214_web.pdf.

CHAPTER 6

1. Robert Safian, "How CEO Mark Parker Runs Nike To Keep Pace With Rapi Change," *Fast Company*, November 5, 2012, https://www.fastcompany. com/3002642/how-ceo-mark-parker-runs-nike-keep-pace-rapid-change.

2. New Plastics Economy, "Global Commitment," accessed January 28, 2020, https://www. newplasticseconomy.org.

3. Frans Johansson, *The Medici Effect: Breakthrough Insights at the Intersection of Ideas, Concepts, and Cultures.* Brighton, MA: Harvard Business Review Press, 2004.

4. Santiago Rincón-Gallardo and Michael Fullan, "Essential Features of Effective Networks in Education," *Journal of Professional Capital and Community*, 2016. Egon Endres, "Grenzgänger—ein neuer Managementtypus," *Internationale Zeitschrift für Veränderung, Lernen, Dialog*, Heft 7, pp. 54–61, 2004.

5. Tamarack Institute, tamarack community.ca, accessed January 28, 2020, www.tamarackcommunity.ca.

6. John Kania and Michael Kramer, "Collective Impact," *Stanford Social Innovation Review*, Winter 2011.

7. Röchling Foundation and Wider Sense, "POLYPROBLEM," 2019, https://www.roechling-stiftung.de/studie-polyproblem.

CHAPTER 7

1. Consultant Bill Hennessy makes a point that Drucker may have never said this quote: Bill Hennessy, "I Wish Drucker Never Said It," September 9, 2015, http://billhennessy.com/simple-strategies/2015/09/09/i-wish-drucker-never-said-it.

2. Peter F. Drucker (1967). *The Effective Executive*, Harper & Rowe, 1967.

3. Paul Brest, *"The* Power of Theories of Change,"
Stanford Social Innovation Review, Spring 2010.

4. Mondelēz International Inc., "Impact for Growth:
2017 Progress Report," p. 36.

5. There are a variety of introductory guides available for
the IOOI method, including "Corporate Citizenship:
plan and measure with the IOOI method: a guide
to the social engagement of companies," from the
Bertelsmann Foundation.

6. Celia Moore, "IBM's Model for Corporate
Philanthropy," *Alliance*, June 1, 2006, https://www.
alliancemagazine.org/feature/ibm-s-model-for-
corporate-philanthropy.

7. MDRC, "An Overview of the NYC P-TECH Grades
9–14 Model," December 2018, https://www.mdrc.
org/publication/overview-nyc-p-tech-grades-9-14-
model.

8. Schneider Electric, "Financial and Sustainable
Development Annual Report: Registration Document
2017," p. 131ff.

9. Jeremy Nicholls et al., *A guide to social return on
investment.* The SROI Network, January 2012, http://
www.socialvalueuk.org/app/uploads/2016/03/The%20
Guide%20to%20Social%20Return%20on%20
Investment%202015.pdf.

10. The B Impact Assessment, accessed January 28,
2020, https://bimpactassessment.net.

11. Economy for the Common Good, accessed January 28, 2020, https://www.ecogood.org/.

12. SASB, accessed January 28, 2020, https://www.sasb.org.

13. Value Balancing Alliance (2019): https://www.value-balancing.com/.

14. The historian Jerry Z. Mueller describes, in detail, when measurement makes sense and when not to do it in his 2018 book, *The Tyranny of Metrics*.

CHAPTER 8

1. This describes the company's old campus. It just moved to a new, purpose-built campus in Dortmund, which is the city next to Witten.

CONCLUSION

1. "Don't do it: Nike is embroiled in a doping scandal," *The Economist*, October 5, 2019, https://www.economist.com/business/2019/10/05/nike-is-embroiled-in-a-doping-scandal.

2. Knut Bergmann and Michael Alberg-Seberich, "Unternehmen dürfen nicht altruistisch sein," Michael Hüther, Knut Bergmann, Dominik H. Enste (Hrsg.), *Unternehmen im öffentlichen Raum*, Springer-Verlag, 2014, pp. 229–250.

INDEX

. . . .

ABOUT THE AUTHORS

DERRICK FELDMANN

Derrick Feldmann is a sought-after speaker, researcher, and advisor for causes and companies on social movements and issue engagement. He regularly speaks at events and organizations around the world on how causes and companies can drive public interest in social change. He is the author of two books, *Social Movements for Good: How Companies and Causes Create Viral Change* and *Cause for Change: The Why and How of Nonprofit Millennial Engagement.*

Feldmann is the managing director of movement design studio INFLUENCE|SG, where he advises companies and causes through research on social issue engagement. He also serves as managing director of Ad Council Edge, the strategic consulting division of the Ad Council.

Feldmann has been recognized as a leading researcher in cause engagement for more than a decade. His work is regularly cited by such outlets as *Forbes, Fast Company,* and *The Wall Street Journal,* and as a reliable source of data on today's cause engagement. He led the research team for *Influencing Young America to Act,* a study of how young adults are influenced by and influence others to support social movements. Prior to that, he led the research team for the Millennial Impact Project for ten years, producing the comprehensive *Millennial Impact Reports* on how the generation has engaged with causes from varying perspectives.

Feldmann is a guest lecturer for the Indiana University O'Neill School of Public and Environmental Affairs and on the board of visitors for the Lilly Family School of Philanthropy at Indiana University.

Author photography by Silke Mayer

MICHAEL ALBERG-SEBERICH

As managing director of Wider Sense, based in Berlin, Michael Alberg-Seberich is responsible for the development of the company. He leads the advisory work of Wider Sense and deals with all questions concerning philanthropy, CSR, and impact investing.

In addition to his consulting activities, Alberg-Seberich works as an organizational developer, facilitator, mediator, and coach. He is a regular contributor to *Alliance* magazine, The Center for Effective Philanthropy blog, and a number of other blogs. Together with the Wider Sense team, he curates and hosts the Wider Sense podcast from the field. He also lectures on a variety of topics in the sector.

Before joining Wider Sense, Alberg-Seberich worked in various senior positions at Active Philanthropy and the Bertelsmann Foundation. At the latter, he was project manager in the field of democracy, human rights, and tolerance education, and led projects on federalism reform and strategy development in politics. He managed and directed the 2007 Carl Bertelsmann Prize, "Social Commitment as an Educational Objective."

Alberg-Seberich studied North American studies, anthropology, and international law at the University of Bonn and the University of British Columbia in Vancouver, Canada. After graduation, he taught languages and cultural policy at the University of Oxford.